Contentment and the Pursuit of Ambition:

The Grattans and Their Remarkable Women

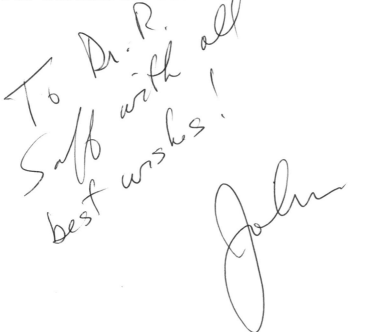

John T. Foster Jr. & Sarah Whitmer Foster

Printed in the U.S.A.

Library of Congress Control Number: 2011943290

ISBN: 978-1-935921-26-4

Dedication:

There are two people who made this book possible.
It is dedicated to them:

Martha, "Marty," Townes Grattan

George G. Grattan IV

Contents:

Photographs   *Page*

Preface

Contentment and The Pursuit of Ambition offers a story of a family of women on a grand scale. For several generations an extended family, the Grattans, produced strong women with two of them selecting husbands who became governors. To insure their family's success, daughters and nieces engaged in business, made economic decisions, and one even set the social calendar of a governor. Before this history ends, Civil War generals organized a Southern army on the family's land. For several days the Grattans watched thousands of men prepare their estate to be a battlefield. Gun batteries could be seen from the windows of their home. Historical events can be more dramatic than fictional events in *Gone With the Wind*.

In 1761, a Scotch-Irish family, the Grattans, purchased land on a major tributary of the Shenandoah River and expected that their efforts in a new land would fulfill their ambitions. Toward this end, they eventually named their home Contentment. They also applied the name to their property, which quickly grew to hundreds of acres on the North River, much of it along the valley turnpike—the forerunner of which carried countless settlers from Pennsylvania and Maryland into the mountains of Tennessee and the Piedmont of the Carolinas.

The Grattans, according to Virginia historian C. E. May, were "important in the history of our ... state and nation." This family, who lived at Contentment, produced a "person of distinction" in four consecutive generations.[1] The Grattans also shared characteristics with many early settlers of the Shenandoah Valley, being Scotch-Irish Protestants who had come to North America for economic reasons. The Grattans, however, differed from other families in the Shenandoah Valley in the scale of their possessions. Their farm and holdings were three times the size of the average Valley farm of the period. Even so they did not believe agriculture alone would produce the affluence they hoped for, and they consequently also engaged in milling, selling trade goods, and practicing law.

While the social prominence of the Grattan family could be attributed to their economic endeavors and their emphasis on education, that would leave out a crucial aspect of their lives. Much of the family's success came from the women and the unusually bold activities in which they engaged. This became clear when the Grattan Family Papers were matched to an antebellum book, *Sketches of Some of the First Settlers of Upper Georgia*. The Grattan Family Papers themselves were mostly manuscripts inherited by George G. Grattan IV and were organized by his wife, Martha, "Marty," Townes Grattan and by Frances Lewis Roller Grattan. In addition, both of these women also located copies of documents, letters, photographs, and created genealogical charts.

When former Georgia governor George Rockingham Gilmer published *Sketches of Some of the First Settlers of Upper Georgia* in 1855, he made a lasting contribution to his state's history. His primary objective at that time was to write about the early settlement of upper Georgia, the area of Athens and Lexington. Since many of these families originally came from Virginia, Gilmer traced them through generations. His book included a section on his wife, Elizabeth or Eliza Frances, who was a Grattan and his first cousin. The publication of *Sketches of Some of the First Settlers of Upper Georgia* created a furor, since the author combined blunt honesty with a rich sense of humor. Many prominent people responded by buying copies and burning them. This only amused George Gilmer, a man accustomed to controversy, and the response enhanced his reputation. One historian observed, "Though he had been prominent in state affairs, it was as the author of this book that he came to be best known." [2]

It is clear in the Grattan papers that George Gilmer's wife, Eliza Frances, was an active participant in creating his book. She gathered information, seeking it even from a cousin in Florida, John G. Gamble. His son later recalled, "A Mrs. Gilmer, who my father...addresses as Cousin Bess," collected "material for certain memoirs, which were afterwards... published by her husband."[3] Gamble responded to Eliza's request by writing descriptions of his parents and grandfather. Eliza also asked her brother at Contentment for historical information. This is not surprising since Robert Grattan Jr. and his wife were in "constant" interaction with the Gilmers by "both letters and visits."[4] Perhaps to the Gilmers' surprise, Robert briefly described his family's origins and launched into a lengthy autobiography—a surviving version stretches to thirty-six pages.

After getting historical information from John Gamble and Robert Grattan, the Gilmers used it sparingly. By doing this, the role of women in the story of the family's success became muted. It was a goal of the present authors of this book to use these materials in a new way, giving voice to the silent. The missing historical information not only provides remarkable insights into the activities of women but it also documents how those activities began. Understanding the life of Catherine Grattan Gamble is crucial, for she was easily one of C.E. May's "persons of distinction."[5] Having come to America as a child of eight in 1759, her knowledge was central to the success of the family's businesses. The skills Catherine learned went far beyond bookkeeping and she evidently taught them to at least one of her daughters. When Catherine was in her seventies, Robert Grattan Jr. found her surrounded by younger men seeking her business advice.[6]

Grattan women followed Catherine's example to chart their own lives, departing from regional trends.[7] In New England during this time, women's primary sphere of influence was the home. The world outside the home—business, politics, and writing—typically became the province of their husbands, fathers, and brothers. By using Catherine Grattan as an example, her daughters and a niece thus liberated themselves to pursue interests far beyond the home. Daughter Elizabeth wrote a successful book before the Civil War, managed the finances of her husband's law firm, and as a widow converted an undeveloped cotton plantation in Florida into a source of wealth. Her cousin, Eliza Frances Grattan Gilmer, charted her husband's social activities and offered suggestions on political decisions.

In the South and elsewhere, marriages based upon romantic love between equals came into vogue in the early republic, 1800–20.[8] Both of Catherine's daughters and Eliza Frances selected their own husbands, pursuing this ideal. Rather than having to experiment with a social unknown, they fortunately could rely upon the successful model of Catherine and her sisters, their aunts, from the 1770s and 1780s. Catherine Grattan had rejected a marriage arranged by her father and publicly embarrassed him in the process. Father John Grattan responded by refusing to grant her permission to marry for a decade. Catherine, however, did prevail and married her beau, Robert Gamble. This process repeated itself, with Catherine's sisters each finding a potential husband, only for her choice to be rejected by John Grattan. Yet all of these women won, with the youngest waiting until John Grattan signed his will, then marrying her love a week later.

It is believed from many sources that patriarchy persisted in the South longer than in other places.[9] John Grattan was every inch a patriarch—he was a remote, aloof Presbyterian with an aristocratic demeanor and dress. As a formidable Scotch-Irishman, he was matched in feuds with daughters who were half Scotch-Irish and half Scottish.

Having rejected a patriarchal model in the 1770s and 1780s, Grattan women chose husbands who would be partners. Having become successful in business at Contentment, Catherine persuaded husband Robert Gamble to sell his farm at the end of the American Revolution. The couple used the funds to establish a successful store in Staunton, Virginia, and then in Richmond. Robert and Catherine would achieve wealth, using it to buy a house designed by Benjamin Latrobe. Following Catherine's example, her two daughters and a niece would marry men receptive to their suggestions and willing to let their wives use their diverse talents. The success of William H. Cabel, George R. Gilmer, and William Wirt cannot be explained without taking into account the influence of their wives and Catherine Grattan.

Although they daringly rejected patriarchy while enhancing their husband's careers, Grattan women evidently were not denied entry to elite social groups. William H. Cabel became Governor of Virginia, Gilmer won the governorship of Georgia twice, and William Wirt served as Attorney General of United States in two separate administrations. It appears that the women suffered no negative consequences at all. On the contrary, the most daring of them, Catherine Grattan Gamble, socialized among Richmond's elite and counted Chief Justice John Marshall among her friends.[10]

Although clearly scholarship will benefit most greatly from the insights in these pages about women, it is also true that the authors were attracted to the Grattan Family Papers for other reasons. As they told their own story, the Grattans differ from many other prominent Virginians. Edward E. Baptist, in his *Creating an Old South,* describes Southerners from the Old Dominion dominating much of the Tallahassee region of Florida. In the 1850s, many such people wrote family histories stressing links to Tidewater Cavaliers and to a European feudal world. These histories project a world of happy slaves, loyal and subservient yeoman farmers, and loving, meek wives—all under the leadership of wise male aristocrats. Our primary sources did not describe the Grattans in such mythical terms. Catherine Grattan could never be described as meek, given her feud with her father alone. The Grattans believed there could be good slave masters, saying that an uncle was one; they did not, however, make this claim for themselves. If they had a loving slave, the Grattans did not reveal it. In the same way, it would have been a fantastic leap to describe Scotch-Irish and

Mennonite neighbors as compliant serfs. Robert Grattan Jr., George R. Gilmer, and John G. Gamble did not engage in any such pretense. The records of the Grattans seem to be creditable.

The content of the Grattan Family Papers also suggested a different use. Through retelling the experiences of the four generations that lived at Contentment, the Grattan story becomes a history of the Shenandoah Valley in miniature. Being prominent in the Shenandoah Valley gave its family members unusual opportunities. Unlike the thousands of men and women who merely saw Stonewall Jackson ride past, Charles Grattan actually interacted with the famous commander, recording his own observations about him. In writing his prizewinning biography, *Stonewall Jackson: the Man, the Soldier and the Legend*, James I. Robertson Jr. needed a description of the future general at Harpers Ferry at the beginning of the Civil War. He turned to Charles Grattan.[11] Decades earlier Charles's grandfather interacted with both Henry "Light Horse Harry" Lee, Robert E. Lee's father, and George Washington. Grattan grandsons in the Civil War copied the behavior of their grandfather who had watched both Lee and Washington. Grattans became captains and majors rather than generals. In politics, they sat in the state house of representatives (House of Delegates). Their chances of having been elected to higher state positions had been lessened by living in the western, less populated part of the state.

It is obvious that the Grattans witnessed American history firsthand, participating in a host of crucial events. These began with the Ulster migration and the American Revolution and continued through the Civil War and the fusion politics of the late nineteenth century. Although the Grattan family history conveys the experiences of an affluent Shenandoah family over a vast length of time, their story is not limited to the Valley. Being Scotch-Irish Presbyterians rather than German Anabaptists, they shared characteristics with leaders in the Piedmont of the Carolinas and Georgia. Before the Civil War, Grattan men were already attending the University of Virginia—a tradition shared with some prominent Scotch-Irish leaders further south.

While it became a goal of the authors to update the family's history and to place it in a local and regional context, the Grattan story can be read for a variety of purposes. For some it traces the lives of remarkable women, and for others it traces a family's journey to understand a very important part of the South. Beyond this work, readers should remember that many Grattans lived in a physical setting that still exists.

Contentment, the house, remains a vivid reflection of their

aspirations, and in many major ways it stands as they built it. The dwelling is in Federal style with refined details—eight fireplaces with eight different mantels—on a large scale. The bricks in exterior walls were laid in a distinctive pattern, Flemish bond. The house chimneys at the gable ends tower some fifty feet above the ground. These are connected, on the opposite sides, by brick cornices, a feature occasionally seen on such buildings. For a number of generations of Americans, Contentment would have approximated a grand house. "Contentment" then, is both a state of mind, reached when the American dream is fulfilled, and a place. Contentment, the house, still stands on a small knoll near the North River. The Blue Ridge Mountains line the horizon some fifteen miles to the east, and the Alleghenies begin ten miles west. Contentment abides in the middle of the Shenandoah Valley—one of the great valleys of America.

Notes:

1. May, "The Grattans in Augusta and Rockingham Counties."

2. *Dictionary of American Biography*, Vol. 7, 307.

3. Gamble, "Reminiscences of Major John Grattan," 1.

4. Grattan, "Manuscript of Major Robert Grattan Jr.," 15.

5. The spelling of Catherine's name varies in colonial records. "Catharine" seems as frequent as "Catherine." Historian C.E. May preferred the latter while in recent times Anya Jabour used the former. It is telling that her son used "Catherine" and that is written on her tombstone.

6. Grattan, 13.

7. A primary one appears in the works of Harriet Beecher Stowe's well-known sister, Catharine Beecher. She stressed the theme of women and improvements in the home. Others have broadened this to male and female areas of influence. Please see Kathryn Kish Sklar's *Catharine Beecher: A Study in American Domesticity* and Carroll Smith-Rosenberg's *Disorderly Conduct: Visions of Gender in Victorian America*.

8. Carl N. Degler, *At Odds: Women and the Family in America from the Revolution To the Present* and Jan Lewis's "The Republican Wife: Virtue and Seduction in the Early Republic," *William and Mary Quarterly*. A more recent study is Anya Jabour's *Marriage in the Early Republic: Elizabeth and William Wirt and Companionate Ideal*.

9. For studies that document male patriarchy in the South, please see Kenneth S. Greenberg's *Masters and Statesmen: the Political Culture of American Slavery* and Steven M. Stowe's *Intimacy and Power in the Old South: Ritual in the Lives of the Planters*.

10. Palmer, Vera. "Gambles Hill: A Rebirth of an Elegant Richmond." Richmond: Albermarle Paper Company, 1962.

11. Robertson, *Stonewall Jackson*, 231. Charles Grattan's descriptive ability was shared by a younger brother: "I was over at Gen. Stuart's this evening and General Beauregard was there. It was the first time I had ever been close to him. He [Beauregard] is [a] very small looking man [who] looks something like an organ grinder all except his eye which is very striking." Robert R. Grattan to Mary E. Grattan, Dec. 7, 1861.

Acknowledgments

There are four people who always expressed an unflagging belief in the value of this work:

Canter Brown Jr.

Roxane Fletcher

Ann Miller Riccardi

Louise Cash Whitmer

GRATTAN FAMILY TREE

FIRST GENERATION
Parents

SECOND GENERATION
Children

THIRD GENERATION
Grandchildren

JOHN GRATTAN***
|
ELIZABETH BROWN

CATHERINE GRATTAN
|
ROBERT GAMBLE

JOHN GRATTAN GAMBLE
|
Robert B. Gamble

ANGES (NANCY) S. B. GAMBLE
|
WILLIAM H. CABELL

JOHN GRATTAN JR.

ELIZABETH GRATTAN
|
Samuel Brown

ELIZABETH WASHINGTON GAMBLE
|
WILLIAM WIRT

JANE GRATTAN

ANGES (NANCY) GRATTAN
|
Elijah Poage

MARGARET LAW GRATTAN
|
Samuel Miller

ELIZABETH (Eliza, Betty) F. GRATTAN
|
GEORGE R. GILMER

ROBERT GRATTAN SR.***
|
Elizabeth T. Gilmer

ROBERT GRATTAN JR.***
|
MARTHA (PATSY) MINOR***

PEACHY RIDGWAY GRATTAN

GRATTAN FAMILY TREE

Only the most important family members are listed. The three youngest children of Robert Grattan Sr., and the two youngest of Robert Jr. have been dropped. They are little more than names. It should be noted that William H. Cabell served as Governor of Virginia and George R. Gilmer served as Governor of Georgia on two separate occasions. William Wirt was, of course, Attorney General of the United States.

The asterisks (***) indicate owners of Contentment. The family chart omits family members that moved away from Virginia. For example, since John Grattan Gamble moved to Florida his children are omitted. The only great-grandchildren listed are those of Robert Grattan Jr.'s

FOURTH GENERATION

Great-Grandchildren

CHARLES GRATTAN
 —
 Elizabeth Crawford Finley

LUCY GILMER GRATTAN
 —
 George D. Chrisman

GEORGE GILMER GRATTAN***
 —
 Mary Ella Heneberger

ROBERT RIDGWAY GRATTAN

PETER MINOR GRATTAN

MARY ELIZABETH GRATTAN
 —
 James F. Robertson

A Place in Time

My grandfather lived on the Shenandoah River—a favorite resort of the white heron—one of whom,...passed by the house, to avoid going round a great bend, and stopped on the house-top to take its direction.[1]

George R. Gilmer, Lexington, Georgia, 1855

The Shenandoah Valley was once a special part of the American frontier. As the famous historian Frederick Jackson Turner put it, the Valley was a portion of the "Old West." For decades in the eighteenth century, a "generation of settlers poured along this mountain trough into the southern uplands or the Piedmont." The Valley of Virginia served as a geological roadway into the interior, and Turner claimed that a "moving mass" of settlers took it. Among them were "the ancestors of John C. Calhoun, Abraham Lincoln, Jefferson Davis, Stonewall Jackson, James K. Polk, Sam Houston, and Davy Crockett."[2]

In 2000, two historians wrote that settlers "began to push into the backcountry, down [or up using traditional usage] the great Shenandoah Valley, running southwest along the eastern flank of the Appalachians. This was the first of the great pioneer treks that took Americans into the continental interior, and the Shenandoah became the site of America's first 'west.' Within a generation settlers could be found all along the front range of the Appalachians, from Pennsylvania south to the Carolina backcountry."[3]

A century later, the Shenandoah Valley returned to national importance during the Civil War. Because it runs from the northeast to the southwest, the Valley offered the Confederacy marked tactical advantages. Military forces could emerge from it to threaten Washington, D.C., or nearby places, as did Thomas "Stonewall" Jackson in 1862 and Jubal Early in 1864. For Southerners, the Shenandoah Valley proved to be a place to attract Union forces, drawing them away from other fronts. Beyond these strategic implications, the Valley's farms were a major source of supplies for Lee's army; for years, it was a primary "breadbasket" of the Confederacy.

Within this context, Thomas "Stonewall" Jackson enlarged the scope of his fame. In the spring of 1862, he outmaneuvered three different armies and initiated a half-dozen engagements from Winchester in the north to the mountains west of Staunton.[4] In the process, he damaged the military reputations of three opposing commanders.[5] After these remarkable achievements, Jackson joined Robert E. Lee's efforts to drive General George B. McClellan away from Richmond. Later in the war, the devastation of the Shenandoah Valley would become a precursor to twentieth-century conflict. Realizing the economic significance of the Valley to Lee's army, General Ulysses S. Grant issued a famous (or infamous) order to Philip Sheridan in 1864 to wage war on the Valley's farmers by burning their barns and slaughtering their livestock. Federal troops thus put an end to the Shenandoah Valley serving as a source of military supplies, foreshadowing the "scorched earth" policies of more recent wars.

These events occurred in a geographically extraordinary place. The Shenandoah Valley runs for more than 120 miles along the northwest border of Virginia. The Valley lies between the Blue Ridge Mountains on the east and the much more rugged Alleghenies to the west. The middle third of the Valley is divided in half lengthwise by a steep, rocky ridge that parallels the larger mountains in both directions. Consequently, the Shenandoah River has two major branches that draw water from both sides of the central ridge. The north and south forks of the river join each other near Front Royal and flow northward to the Potomac, meeting it at Harpers Ferry. For early settlers, it was easy to enter the Valley from Pennsylvania since the mountains did not present a major obstacle coming from the north. Once inside in the Shenandoah Valley, settlers often traveled "up" it and then continued south into related valleys, or crossed back over the Blue Ridge into the Piedmont.

The Shenandoah Valley and the Shenandoah River are, of course, recognized for their remarkable beauty. In the 1930s, a national park was created on the adjacent Blue Ridge Mountains to help preserve the area for generations to come. What is less widely known is the Valley's importance in American history, as the events rivaled the physical setting for drama. The following account begins before the arrival of the Grattans on Virginia's frontier in 1761 and ends shortly after the beginning of the twentieth century, covering major periods in the Valley's history and that of the United States as well.

Notes:

1. Gilmer, *Sketches of Some of the First Settlers of Upper Georgia*, 449.

2. Turner, *The Frontier in American History*, 99, 105.

3. Hine and Faragher, *The American West: a New Interpretive History*, 77.

4. See page 415 in Robertson. "With Fremont swinging up from the south, Shields with two more divisions coming in from the east, and Banks possibly able to initiate a second southward push, Federal pressure would be like a giant pincer on Jackson's outnumbered band."

5. Based upon page 446 in Robertson's *Stonewall Jackson*. "Banks [Nathaniel P.], wearing the stigma of a loser, would mark time while other generals moved past him up the military ladder, Shields [James] quickly faded from view as a Union commander. When a junior officer was given command of a new Union army, Fremont [John C.] angrily resigned his commission."

(1.) 3d Corps, May 8th
(2.) 3d Corps, May 9th
(3.) 3d Corps, May 10th and 11th
(4.) Stuart checked Federal advance night of May 7th

2D CORPS, A.N.VA.,
May 3d, 1864,
AND THE
ROUTES OF MARCH
from May 4th to May 21st, 1864,
TO
BATTLES OF THE WILDERNESS
AND
SPOTSYLVANIA C.H., VA.
To accompany Report of
JED. HOTCHKISS, Top. Eng. V.D.

Scale : 160.000

REFERENCE.
—— Confederate

0 ½ 1 2 3 4 5 6 7 8 9 10 Miles.

Accompanying report of Capt. Jed Hotchkiss, C.S.Army
Top Engineer 2d Corps A.N.V. (Valley District.)
SERIES I VOL. XXXVI PART I

Nº 11.
MAP
SHOWING
ROUTES AND CAMPS
OF THE
ARMY OF THE VALLEY DIST.
FROM
STAUNTON, VA., TO WASHINGTON, D.C.,
AND BACK TO
STRASBURG, VA.,
from June 27th to July 22d, 1864.,
to accompany Report of
JED. HOTCHKISS, Top. Eng. A.V.D.

Scale of Miles.

0   10   20   30   40

REFERENCES.
Cavalry Routes -----
Infantry do ——
Camps ▲▲
Confederate

V I R G I N ...

Hagerstown
Williamsport
Boonsborough
Falling Water
North Depot
July 4th
Martinsburg
July 3d
Shepherdstown
Crampton's Gap
Darkesville
Bunker Hill
Leetown
A July 3d Brown
White Hall
Smithfield
Md. Hts.
Bracetown
Cameron
Charlestown
Rutherfords
Stephenson's
Summit Point
Winchester
July 20th
Kernstown
Berryville
Cool Spg.
July 18th
Hillsborough
Newtown
Bartonsville
Millwood
Purcellville
Leesburg
Double Toll Gate
White Post
Snicker's Gap
Middletown
July 20th
Berry's Fy.
Cedarville
Strasburg
Hill Buckton
Ashby's Gap
Maurertown
Front Royal
MANASSAS GAP R.R.
Yal. View
Woodstock
Chester Gap
Edenburg
Hundurstown
Milford
Rude's Hill
Luray
Brock's Gap
New Market
Timberville
Tenth Legions
Sparta
June 29th
Big Spring (Lacey's)
Big Spr.
Harrisonburg
Dayton
Keezletown
Conrad's Store
Bridgewater
Mt. Crawford
Mossy Cr.
Parnassus
Spring Hill
Churchville
Mt. Sidney
Swoope's
Staunton
Hermitage
Fishersville
Waynesborough
Greenwood
Rockfish Gap
Jarman's Gap
Brown's Gap
Swift Run Gap
Rockfish Mills
Port Republic
Weyer's Cave
Mt. Meridian
New Hope
Christian's Cr.
VA. CENTRAL

5.
Mt. Jackson
(massed)
Mt. Airy (Meem)
Locust Grove
Rev. A.R. Rude
—— Confederate
—— Federal
Nº 99.
WICKHAM'S ATTACK ON FED. CAV.,
Nov. 22d, 1864.

Accompanying Journal of Capt Jed Hotchkiss, C.S.Army,
Top Engineer 2d Corps, A.N.V. (Valley District.)
SERIES I VOL. XLIII. PART I

Accompanying report of Capt. Jed Hotchkiss, C.S.Army
Top Engineer 2d Corps, A.N.V. (Valley District.)
SERIES I VOL. XXXVII PART I

1. Pioneers in the Shenandoah Valley: 1759–1773

The Grattans left Belfast in 1759, sailed across the Atlantic Ocean, and disembarked in Philadelphia. Although they were able to come as regular passengers rather than in steerage, as scores of other immigrants to American did, the journey would have nonetheless been difficult. The parents, John and Elizabeth Brown Grattan, were accompanied by many of their children. The eldest, Catherine, was only eight years old. Next in age came a son, John, followed by daughters Elizabeth, Jane, and Nancy. Of the children, Jane's handicaps added worry since, "She [had] received an injury during her infancy, which affected her mind, and from which she never recovered."[1]

The arrival of a Scotch-Irish family in Philadelphia in the 1750s was by then commonplace. There had already been waves of emigrants from Ulster, driven to North America by exorbitant rents and a series of devastating crop failures. An observer noted, "When the fourth successive year of drought ruined the crops in 1717, serious preparations began to be made for migration. Ships were chartered, consultations were held, groups were organized, and property was sold. More than five thousand Ulstermen that year made the journey to the American colonies."[2] This same process repeated itself almost a decade later when an archbishop in 1728 wrote, "We have had three bad harvests together. About 4,200 men, women, and children have been shipped off from home...about 3,100 this last summer."[3] However difficult the sea journey for those who left, it was preferable to starving outright. The famine of 1740–41 caused the deaths of an "estimated 400,000 persons." It is not surprising that this produced an exodus to America that lasted for several decades.

As life became episodically more difficult in Ireland, positive reports and messages came from settlers in the New World. The lure of cheap land, vast and fertile, under the control of agreeable local leaders, became ever more attractive. The circulation of good news from America was in the interest of the colonists also. William Penn's efforts to advertise opportunities in Pennsylvania were duplicated by others. In the Shenandoah Valley itself, enormous land grants to William Beverley and Benjamin Borden were made contingent upon their finding settlers. Both men found eager recruiters who journeyed back and forth to Ulster seeking new residents. The powerful combination of economic trouble at home and knowledge of the success abroad affected attitudes about immigration. The desire to leave Ulster in 1728 was described by an observer as spreading "like a contagious distemper."[4]

The Grattans came to Pennsylvania during the French and Indian War, a period (1754-1763) associated with neither a great drought in Ulster nor a wave of major emigration. A grandchild attributed the move to John Grattan and his businesses. "It was understood he left Ireland in bad humor with the government, caused by some injustice which he thought had been done." The injustice probably involved the family's flour mill, which incurred "considerable losses."[5]

Information about the Grattans in Europe is only fragmentary. The family may have originally come from Derbyshire, England, where a prominent Grattan lived in the seventeenth century.[6] It was believed that two brothers moved to Ireland during or after the English Civil War, one settling near Belfast and the other in Dublin.[7] Both men were said to be committed Protestants, and this seems quite likely since the Grattans who came to Philadelphia in 1759 were Presbyterians and their distant cousins in Dublin, including the famous Henry Grattan, remained ardent Protestants. In describing his ancestry in the 1850s, an American member of the family wrote, "The highest patent of nobility our family claimed was our grandfather's dismission [dismissal] from the Presbyterian Church in Ireland as a member in good standing."[8] John Grattan, though, attached little importance to his ancestry. A relative commented, "He [John Grattan] was a man of sense and energy"… who "… relied upon his own exertion for his advancement and respectability in the world." When he was asked by his son Robert about their relationship to Henry Grattan of Ireland, he replied, "Mind, Mind, Bob. Take care of yourself and you will always have kin enough."[9]

When John Grattan arrived in Philadelphia and later in Virginia, he would have been a striking figure in person. One of his relatives noted:

My recollection of the appearance of the old gentleman is, that he was, in person, about five feet eight inches in height, of slender form, fine face, and an address and manner far superior to the rest of the community in which he lived. His manner was aristocratic, and he was conspicuous by neatness in his dress, and the only person, who, in those days, wore a cravat, which was tied in a small bowknot, and the ends fastened in a breast-pin conspicuous on his bosom. Instead of boots, his legs, when riding, were clothed in black leathern gaiters, reaching to the knee, and having a bar of steel passing from knee to ankle through loops instead of buttons.[10]

A different relative wrote, "Though John Grattan's residence was on the frontier, he retained the manners and dress of the old-time gentleman, wearing always a full suit of black, and powdered wig, when he went into company." The writer added, "He is represented as having been about medium size, dark hazel eyes, very handsome and of a...controlling countenance, active on foot and a splendid horse man."[11]

Descriptions of his wife, Elizabeth Brown Grattan, are less detailed. This comes from the fact that she died five to seven years before her husband, and many of her grandchildren had not yet been born. One of the eldest wrote, "[O]ur Grandmother died while I was young, and my recollections of her are very indistinct, further than that she was a kind, motherly-looking old lady."[12] Other relatives comment upon her beauty. "Mrs. Grattan was one of the most beautiful women of the country. She retained until old age the charms which so captivated her husband when he first saw her"—yet this statement comes from a person with little firsthand knowledge. [13]

Elizabeth Brown was born in Scotland about 1730, and her interaction with John Grattan began by chance. "The first act which tradition makes known of John Grattan, was his going into Scotland, and, Irishman-like, falling desperately in love with a beautiful young lady, whom he accidentally met with at a boarding school." The girl's father tried to slow down the relationship, entreating the couple to wait until she finished "her education."[14] But, contrary to her father's wishes, Elizabeth Brown's and John Grattan's courtship continued, leading to their early marriage. Several humorous stories, as we shall see, remain about Elizabeth Brown Grattan, suggesting that she brought to her family a liveliness that counterbalanced the personality of her austere, driven husband.

When the Grattans arrived in Philadelphia, it had a sizeable

Scotch-Irish community. Their move to America may well have come with careful planning and it is likely, given the thousands from Ulster who preceded them, that they already had friends to welcome them. Over the next year, the Grattans remained in Philadelphia, waiting for the war to end and learning firsthand about opportunities in America. It seems probable that visits to Scotch-Irish communities in Pennsylvania were followed with ones to the Shenandoah Valley, because many of the most attractive properties near Philadelphia had already become expensive. As Governor Dobbs of North Carolina recalled in the 1750s, many of the Scotch-Irish moved "southward for want of lands to take up."[15]

Pennsylvania and Virginia were each following different patterns of development. Very early in his efforts, William Penn recognized the need to attract small farmers; consequently, one social historian claimed that "within fifty years of its founding," Penn's "province was full of small farmers from Northern Ireland and Germany."[16] In stark contrast, 150 years of leadership from Tidewater gentry in Virginia had left the Shenandoah Valley empty. "It was only at the beginning of the 18th century that the rulers of Virginia began to think of inviting immigrants into the back-country—and then primarily as a military safeguard."[17] As a new policy emerged among Virginia's leaders, settlers from Pennsylvania were already in Maryland, working their way south.

In 1730, William Gooch, Governor of Virginia, granted 40,000 acres on both sides of the Potomac River to members of the Van Meter family. Within a short period, they resold their land to Joist Hite, who brought German families to Winchester. After this initial success, William Gooch offered even larger tracts in what are now Augusta and Rockingham counties to William Beverley and to Benjamin Borden in 1736. The Beverley parcel amounted to over 118,000 acres "between the great mountains, on the river Sherando [Shenandoah]."[18] In modern terms, this included an area running from Staunton to Waynesboro and northward some miles. Borden, who was an agent for Lord Fairfax, received a tract immediately north of the Beverley estate. Contingent upon this agreement, mentioned earlier, came the stipulation that Borden would settle at least one hundred families. He met the terms of this agreement and received clear title to his land in 1739. The grants to Beverley and Borden came after the arrival of a few Scotch-Irish families. Agents of both Beverley and Borden needed settlers and generally "dealt amicably with those already established upon their land." Consequently, one social historian believed that many early families "took pains to have their lands surveyed and their purchases confirmed."[19]

The Shenandoah Valley offered attractions to settlers that rivaled those of southeastern Pennsylvania. According to one historian, "Most of the Valley of Virginia was a vast prairie, showing to pioneers a vista of fertile territory, making settlement easy and rapid. The Indians, who used the whole valley for hunting, had created the prairie. At the close of each hunting season, they set fire to open ground, thus keeping it from reverting to woodland. This was done to attract the buffalo, an animal that shunned forest and lived on grasslands."[20] And although the Valley served as a hunting preserve for Native Americans, it was not regarded as the possession of any particular tribe. Thus, while early settlers occasionally interacted with members of different Native American groups, they met little organized resistance.

In the two decades following the legalization of the Beverly and Borden grants in the 1730s, hundreds of Scotch-Irish families settled on their tracts. The area rapidly became a center of settlement for them. As a social historian observed, "Two counties in the Valley of Virginia, Augusta and Rockingham, claim to be the most Scotch-Irish counties in the present United States. It is said that they have more Presbyterians within their borders than members of all other denominations together."[21] A preliminary visit to the Valley in 1760 by the Grattans would have confirmed the region as one of great opportunity, held by an ever-growing Ulster community. A German community was also present but it was outnumbered by their English-speaking neighbors. Beyond farming, the limited number of stores and mills suggested potential for establishing more for the future. Milling already existed but its quality seems to have lagged behind that of other regions.

On the 17th of February 1761, John Grattan purchased 156 acres on North River, a major tributary of the South Fork of the Shenandoah River, from John Camplin [Johannes Keplinger] and Lydia Camplin [Keplinger]. The Camplins had obtained this parcel from Benjamin Borden's agents on the 7th of August 1757. To his holdings, John Grattan added two adjacent tracts on August 18, 1766, buying them from the Bordens. The first consisted of 235 acres and the second of an additional 185. By making this new purchase for 120 pounds sterling, Grattan had created the nucleus of his holdings.[22]

These purchases reflected great care in their selection. The land lay on the North River with its deep channel, which offered a continuous stream of waterpower for a mill and a means of transporting barrels of grain. Meanwhile, through the middle of the property ran the main trail through the Shenandoah Valley. Along it came a constant flow of new settlers heading to the frontier. As they passed the Grattans, merchandise could be sold to them from a store. The attractive combination, including rich river bottomland for farming, indicated a property with extraordinary promise. John and Elizabeth Grattan realized that this could well be the place to actualize their dreams of worldly success. In time, their family named their home "Contentment," no doubt fully expecting that their insight, industry, and faith would make the location a true Promised Land.

In the period of the Camplins' ownership, they had placed several fields into cultivation and built a modest log cabin. This gave John and Elizabeth Grattan a home to bring their children to in the spring of 1761. Once on their new farm, the Grattans began adapting it to their needs, opening a store. As a grandson recalled, John Grattan "embarked in merchandise, and considering the sparse population of that part of the country, did a large business; collecting his debts in the shape of cattle, which found their market in Philadelphia."[23] Still another relative added that he was a merchant supplying "foreign goods" to "that part of the valley" where the "great road from the west to the north crosses the Shenandoah River."[24]

Without even a teenage child, the Grattans had little choice but to hire workers for the construction of the store, in digging a lengthy millrace, and assembling a gristmill. One grandson believed that his grandfather's projects meant that he was "surrounded by a number of dependent mechanics, laborers, &c., many of whom were German."[25] Catherine's interaction with workers who practiced Freemasonry also indicates the varied background of the employees. The prank she played on them, as we shall see, is the handiwork of a teenager. This would suggest the mill project lagged the opening of the store by perhaps four or five years. The objective in this case would have been to own the best—a thought confirmed by their grandchildren. One declared it to be "the first good manufacturing flour mill in the Shenandoah" while another believed it had "the first burr mill stone" west of the Blue Ridge.[26] By the close of the 1760s, the Grattans held a productive farm of almost 600 acres, a thriving store, and a mill that produced quality flour.

Credit for these achievements belonged not only to John and Elizabeth but also to their children. While it is unlikely that women from proper Scotch-Irish families worked in the fields, social class distinctions did not limit them to the household. As a child, Catherine Grattan probably faced a long list of chores, from cooking and washing clothes to making butter. When time permitted, she played with local children, not sharing the aloof nature of her father. "This aristocratic feeling...did not so pervade the younger members of the family as to prevent them from forming and keeping up friendly relations with all around them, of decent behavior and good character." Catherine's son recalled a crucial development: "Many of the neighbors and also the employees about [the] farm and homestead were Germans, then called Dutch, which enabled my dear mother to acquire such a knowledge of their language as was of great advantage to her father in his mercantile business..."[27]

Within a year or two of settling at Contentment, Catherine found herself in the middle of business transactions between her parents and German customers. It was exciting for a child of eleven or twelve to be relieved of household chores to translate the requests of German farmers. An early refrain from John and Elizabeth to their smallest children must have been, "Go find Catherine." "Bring Catherine to the store." As business increased, Catherine found herself in the store, and many of her own household chores were shifted to her younger sisters or to domestic help.

As Catherine's business knowledge increased, she helped her mother on buying trips to purchase merchandise for the store. A relative recalled, "When John Grattan settled in Western Virginia, but little coin circulated there. Trade was managed in the old way of barter. The goods bought of the merchant were paid for in cattle, ginseng, pink-root, and bear and deer skins. These articles were disposed of in Philadelphia. His wife usually transacted this part of John Grattan's business. She went to Philadelphia on horseback, directed the drovers, sold the roots, cattle, and peltries, and bought the goods for her husband's stores. She was frequently accompanied by one of her daughters, most usually Catherine...."[28] Business in Philadelphia took days, and the Grattan women enjoyed staying with old friends. "Friends in the city enabled...." them "...to pass what time they had for pleasure very agreeably in the best society."[29]

Knowledge of Catherine's brother John Grattan Jr., indicates that he too followed his parents in business. The relationship between the oldest children was very close. Catherine's son recalls, "My dear mother loved him with all a sister's heart, and ever spoke of him as her dear brother and friend, whose affection, advice and support she had always experienced."[30] The success of the Grattan store gave rise to a second, located some seventy miles to the southwest at Fincastle. The task of running this establishment came to John Jr. at an early age. Opening the second store required his father's frequent presence and, at the same time, the activities of Catherine grew in importance. By the end of the 1760s, John Grattan Sr. circulated through the Shenandoah Valley, monitoring the family's different enterprises. The Grattans pursued the American dream in multiple avenues.

The work schedule was enlivened with pranks and practical jokes. One from the 1760s would be recorded decades later. Catherine's son explained:

> Among the employees at our Grandfather's were several young men who were, or professed to be, Freemasons, and they now and then held a 'Lodge' in one of the houses which were in the yard enclosing the family dwelling. My mother, who had as merry a temper as any of the family, used to laugh at them and suggest, as their object, the most ridiculous things she could think of—among others that of holding conferences with old Satan, their Master. She would add that she would like to see the old fellow; that she had some questions to ask, to which she would like to hear the answers. Some of the young men at length said that if she was desirous of such an interview they would gratify her, and taking advantage of the absence of her father and mother, on one of their Lodge nights they invited her to attend. She went, and secretly carried in her hand, under her dress, a stout iron poker, to use, if necessary. The night was very dark. She found the room curiously ornamented, and dimly lighted. She and sister were placed at the end opposite the door, a large circle was chalked on the floor within which she and all others in the room were placed; telling her that only within the magic circle would she or even the Masons be safe from the clutches of Old Nick. They commenced the incantations in some gibberish unintelligible to her, and doubtless to themselves. Presently some curious sounds were heard beneath the floor, which, the Masons said, announced the coming of Satan. Some of the fraternity who were not present in the room, caused flashes of light out in the road, by exploding gun powder, and at the same instant a dark figure, with horns on its head, passed the open door. In a few seconds another flash of light and the re-passing of the same figure. At that instant mother rushed forward exclaiming: 'I must speak with his Majesty!' They tried to stop her, but she was too quick. Away ran the Devil, and she close at his heels. He tried to get over the fence, but before he got to the top she had his accoutrements, and so belabored him

with the poker that he was fain to call for mercy. He proved to be one of the Masons, dressed up, with a pair of cow's horns attached to his head-gear. His Majesty carried the marks of the poker for some time... Mother used to say that after she got into the Lodge she felt angry with herself for going, but being in, she [was] determined to see it out.[31]

The other break from work came on the Sabbath, which was strictly observed. The Grattans traveled eight miles "up" the main Valley trail to the Augusta Stone Church. Services at the time went on for three hours, ending before lunch. Since many Presbyterians believed that God attended the prayers, the behavior considered most appropriate was to stand up. Leyburn suggested that "the Scot believed his God preferred a man with self-respect enough to stand in His presence."[32] Still other congregations kneeled, a preference that John Grattan held. The hymns of this period, as one might expect, were also very different from those of today. "In the stricter congregations only Rouse's metrical version of the Psalms was used, and the number of tunes was very limited; the more liberal congregations used not only the Psalms but also Watt's *Hymns and Psalms*. There were no musical instruments of any kind." Since many churches could not afford any psalms or hymnals, an elder "read out a line or two and then led the congregation in singing it; there upon, he recited other lines, and the singing was continued through all the verses."[33] Many Presbyterians continued this practice long after they could have afforded hymnals.

A quiet lunch typically followed the morning service. Then came an afternoon service that repeated the same components as the morning service—a sermon, prayer, Bible reading, and hymns. If this was not enough religious observance, families gathered later in the day for their own private worship. The eldest member of the Grattan family normally insisted on holding Sunday evening prayers with his wife and children. This practice gave rise to a story that was told for generations: "According to the fashion of his people, he prayed long prayers with his family, especially on Sabbath evenings. On one occasion he was unusually prolix [verbose]." When John Grattan got up from his knees, his son "remained in his praying posture." His mother went to the child, "patted him softly on the head, saying, 'Johnny, Johnny! I thought Father Grattan was long enough!'"[34]

In religious affairs the elder John Grattan was a conservative and proud of it. One grandchild recalled, he "was of the old Covenanters' faith and practice. He sung David's Psalms in long metre. Nothing gave him more temper to swear, than to hear in church, upon a sacramental occasion, a Methodist spiritual song sung in short measure."[35]

In the 1760s, the weekly routine was interrupted by the births of two additional children. Elizabeth Brown Grattan gave birth to a fifth daughter, Margaret Law Grattan, and then to her and her husband's amazement, she gave birth to a son, Robert Grattan, in 1769, at Contentment. This ended her known pregnancies, Elizabeth being nearly 40 years of age and her eldest daughter about 18.

While Elizabeth was caring for infant Robert, his father began practicing law. In 1770, John Grattan joined a small group of men who served as justices for Augusta County, an area encompassing both modern Augusta and Rockingham counties, as well as sizeable areas of West Virginia. A term as justice for one year was renewed annually between 1772 and 1776.[36] Taking this task very seriously, John Grattan studied English law. In 1771–1772, he appears among the "subscribers in Virginia" to Blackstone's well-known *Commentaries on the Laws of England.* The other local subscribers included merchants in Staunton, William Bowyer and George Matthews, attorneys in the county, Gabriel Jones and Peter Hog, and surveyor Thomas Lewis.[37] When the American Revolution began, it did not affect John Grattan's position as a county justice. He kept the same position after Rockingham County, his home county, was created out of northern Augusta County late in 1777. This made him, when the new court organized in the following April, one of the new county's first justices, a fact reported by historian John Wayland.[38] Court sessions typically dealt with wills and minor offenses. In the summer of 1778, Rockingham justices heard a murder case, probably its first. "The said Slave Will, being brought to the Bar and arraigned, pleaded he was not guilty." [39] The judges, in turn, examined witnesses, who supported a different conclusion. They claimed the man had "fractured the scull" of Hans Cloverfield with a barrel "stave." John Grattan joined the other judges, finding Will guilty and ordering his execution.

John Grattan also served the county in another role–the vestry. Virginia counties had been organized into Anglican parishes before the Revolution–with lay leaders building chapels, providing for widows and orphans, and protecting public morals. Strange as it may seem, many counties used Presbyterians to perform Anglican duties. The specter of ardent Calvinists taking oaths to serve the Anglican Church, according to the historian C. E. May, seems to have not bothered the Valley folk. Many saw the vestry as a public necessity and concluded that if it existed, it should be controlled by their own. In any case, John Grattan served as a vestryman in 1771, 1778, and 1779. His wife Elizabeth, with her sense of humor, must have watched with amusement as her husband supervised the construction of an Anglican chapel in what is now Dayton, Virginia. After the revolution, without either a congregation or public support, the building became a barn–a situation that probably did not bother the Grattans.[40]

In the early 1770s, Catherine Grattan, still single, was already older than many local women who had a husband and several children. Preoccupied with two stores, a mill, a large farm, and public offices, John Grattan may have pretended not to notice his daughter's social plight. Catherine was invaluable to him. By running a store, translating transactions from German to English, and serving as a buyer with her mother, Catherine was an essential and irreplaceable figure. John Grattan probably loathed the thought of losing her to a husband, and for some years she agreed with him. Becoming a wife on the Colonial frontier would have cost her, at a minimum, those trips to Philadelphia. The person who probably tried to end the conspiracy was Elizabeth, recognizing that her eldest daughter was becoming the oldest unmarried woman in the congregation. In time, Elizabeth forced the matter upon her husband. With this distasteful task in mind, John Grattan looked about the Shenandoah Valley for a man with enough wealth and power. Finding none, he then looked among men his age in Philadelphia, located a widower, and began arranging Catherine's marriage. John's prospective son-in-law decided to visit Contentment, perhaps to settle the agreement. Many upperclass marriages at the time were less "love matches" and more like today's corporate mergers. Hearing the news about the "rich old merchant," Catherine immediately ran "away, and concealed herself in the house of a friend." Wherever the Grattans searched, the young woman could not be found. After several days, the dismayed parents watched the suitor lose "his patience and return home."[41] When it was safe, Catherine Grattan returned to Contentment: clearly she possessed a will equal to her father's, the most formidable of men. A grandson's memories of John Grattan indicate the scale of her victory: "[He] kept his children in great awe, and I well remember when a child having the same feeling towards him; nor have I any recollection of being seated on his knee, or having ever been played with or caressed, as children are wont to be by Grandpapas, and as I feel impelled to play with and caress my Grandchildren."[42]

This unexpected event left John simultaneously livid but in a way relieved. He had lost a rich son-in-law, but this also restored Catherine to her regular duties. In addition, her extraordinary behavior freed her father from the task of finding her another husband. Elizabeth Grattan thus could no longer pressure her husband and he became very pleased with the status quo. Catherine having profoundly embarrassed her father also meant he would refuse any suggestion of marriage his daughter might contemplate. Contemplation did occur in the middle of the 1770s, when Catherine became enamored with Robert Gamble. The Gambles lived in Augusta County, a short distance from the Presbyterian Stone Church. It is even possible that Robert was the reason why Catherine had fled from Contentment.

Family members and many local people knew that John Grattan had refused to give permission to three of his daughters to marry. Records in the nineteenth century indicate some details of the situation: Jane was mentally handicapped, and both Nancy and Margaret clearly received a "No" from their father. These same records do not explain why their sister Elizabeth and Sam Brown obtained John Grattan's consent. Elizabeth's beau was the most improbable man any of the Grattans married on the frontier. Sometime in the aftermath of Catherine's prospective marriage, her sister Elizabeth and Sam Brown came to John Grattan for permission to wed. Under any normal circumstance, an alliance between John Grattan and Samuel Brown would have been unthinkable. Col. Samuel Brown was remembered by one of his grandnephews "as a good natured, indolent man, with little or no energy of character, and apparently indifferent to whether his worldly good increased or not. His ruling passion seemed to be a fondness for the hunter's life, and until too old for such adventures, he annually left his family for six or eight weeks camping in the uninhabited country on the Kanawha and Big Sandy Rivers, amusing himself killing bear and deer, living upon flesh alone, substituting the flesh of deer for bread, while the principal repast was bear's meat."[43] But as a family member, Sam Brown would serve as proof that John Grattan knew best—surely the previously rejected older merchant would seem preferable than the lazy hunter in the eyes of his other daughters. So Grattan said yes and afterwards regretted his rashness. But Sam carried his new wife off to the frontier and the old man was seldom confronted by his mistake.

As years passed, the conflict between John and Catherine Grattan produced an unanticipated result. Catherine's life included a series of funerals for young Colonial women, the girls she had known in the 1760s, many of whom married as teenagers, bore several children, and died of exhaustion before they turned 20 or 25. By staying single, Catherine Grattan remained in fine health, extending her life expectancy beyond many in her generation. Birth and childrearing had no chance to impair her health as a young woman.

A year or so after the marriage of Elizabeth to Sam Brown, the time came for the birth of a baby. Catherine was dispatched to her sister's home with an amazing result: "Col. Brown lived on the frontier, and my mother [reports Catherine's son] had gone there to stay with her sister at the birth of her first child. While there the Indians made an inroad and murdered a neighboring family. The frightened neighbors ran to Brown for protection, because his house was better fitted to resist an attack. This was in the night, and as the Indian party was supposed to be strong, it was important that intelligence should be carried into the more thickly inhabited part of the country, so that relief might be sent, if Brown should be besieged." Decades earlier, Sam's brother had been captured by an Indian raiding party. This incident cast a long shadow over the Brown family, and the prospect of it being repeated terrorized Catherine's sister, Elizabeth. Attempting to calm her, Catherine accepted this challenge—to get help and to carry Elizabeth's child from Green Briar back to the Valley. Catherine's son continues, "My mother undertook to be the messenger, and on horseback, with her sister's infant in her lap, and without other attendant, she rode thirty miles before daylight, over hills and mountains, where, in those days, none other roads than bridle paths had been made."[44]

Catherine's real ride may have been slightly different from this account. It is likely that two or three years passed between the birth of Elizabeth's first child and Catherine's visit. If this were the case, the child would have been a toddler, not an infant—one more likely to remain quiet. And if this timing is actually accurate, then the raid by Native Americans would have occurred shortly after the beginning of the American Revolution.

News of this event traveled and followed Catherine Grattan. The public was in awe of her father because of his distant manner and growing wealth, but her bravery now created her own reputation. The courage of the Scots, the bravery of a Robert the Bruce, were no longer only stories of old—they were personified in this living woman of the Shenandoah Valley. When she said her name in groups of people, heads must have turned. When she was introduced, eyes would widen or stare. So, this is *the* Catherine Grattan! This woman had done the remarkable—she had earned a reputation far outshining most men.

Catherine's status as a formidable celebrity helps explain her relationships with men. Her nephew, Robert Grattan Jr., found distinguished men hovering around her, among them a former governor of Virginia and a nationally recognized author and attorney, William Wirt. Catherine was a central figure in social gatherings—reversing the pattern normal at that time of women hovering around prominent men. Knowledge of Catherine's past also explains events in 1814.[45] When it appeared that British troops would seize Richmond, many affluent males quaked at the prospect. Catherine, on the other hand, remained calm. Given her own military experience, and their lack of it, upper-class men in the city turned to her. While men scrambled to put their affairs in order, they entrusted their families to Catherine. Her nephew wrote, "Many of the gentlemen sent their wives to her house to follow and be guided by her, and she by her coolness and firmness saved them any trouble."[46]

Before turning to that era, a more important conflict was brewing—the American Revolution. While the Grattans were establishing their farm and stores in the Shenandoah Valley, the British government instituted a series of new taxes to pay for the French and Indian War. The Townshend Acts added duties on tea, lead, paper, paint, and other imported commodities. The political repercussions lasted for years, beginning in 1767 and continuing even after the Acts' repeal in 1770. Many Americans resented the tariffs—sentiments that appealed to both Catherine and John Grattan. Having struggled bitterly among themselves over marriage, the Grattan family soon faced national issues that brought them back together.

Notes:

1. The trip across the Atlantic might have occurred, according to family sources, as early as 1758. The French fleet, however, would still have been a menace at that time. This threat became reduced markedly when English admiral Edward Hawke blockaded the port of Brest in May 1759. News of this event signaled that ocean lanes were safer, increasing the likelihood of a relatively safe journey in the summer of 1759. Gamble, "Reminiscences of Major John Grattan," 3.
2. Leyburn, *The Scotch-Irish*, 168.
3. Ibid., 171.
4. Ibid.
5. Gamble, 1.
6. Peachy Ridgway Grattan to John Grattan, Dec. 15, 1879.
7. C.E. May, "The Grattans in Augusta and Rockingham Counties," 1.
8. Grattan, "Manuscript of Major Robert Grattan Jr.," 1.
9. Ibid., 2.
10. Gamble, 1.
11. Grattan, 2.
12. Gamble, 2.
13. Gilmer, *Sketches*, 28.
14. Ibid., 29.
15. Leyburn, 172.
16. Ibid., 200.
17. Ibid., 201.
18. Ibid., 204.
19. Ibid., 205.
20. Ibid., 206.
21. Ibid., 200.
22. Chalkley, *Chronicles of the Scotch-Irish Settlement*, Vol., 3, 366, 448.
23. Gamble, 1.
24. Gilmer, *Sketches*, 26.
25. Gamble, 2.
26. Gilmer, *Sketches*, 27; Grattan, 1.
27. Gamble, 2.
28. Gilmer, *Sketches*, 27.
29. Ibid.
30. Gamble, 4.
31. Ibid., 5.
32. Leyburn, *The Scotch-Irish*, 290.
33. Ibid., 290.
34. Gilmer, *Sketches*, 28.

35. Ibid., 27.

36. Chalkley, *Chronicles of the Scotch-Irish Settlement*, Vol. 1, 160, 166, 170, 175, 177, 183, 188, 189, 196.

37. "Subscribers in Virginia to Blackstone's Commentaries," 184.

38. Wayland, *History of Rockingham County*, 66.

39. "Punishment of a Slave for Murder," 304.

40. C. E. May, *Life Under Four Flags*, 107.

41. Gilmer, *Sketches*, 28.

42. Gamble, "Reminiscences of Major John Grattan," 1.

43. Ibid., 2.

44. Ibid., 4-5. This event is mentioned in other sources, including Alexander Brown's *Cabells and Their Kin*, and Vera Palmer's "Gamble's Hill." Catherine Grattan Gamble "possessed a degree of moral and physical courage equal to any emergency. Once, while living on the frontiers, she rode thirty miles in one night, with her sister's infant in her lap, to notify the settlements of the approach of the Indians." Brown, 257. Also see Gamble, 4-5. Catherine's ride is also described in a microfilm manuscript in the State Library of Florida, Tallahassee.

45. Grattan, "Manuscript of Major Robert Grattan Jr.," 13.

46. Ibid., As her son put it, "My mother possessed great energy and decision of character, and a degree of moral and physical courage equal to any emergency. Her intellect was strong and her judgment of men and things seemed intuitive. Evidence of all this was seen in the influence she exerted over all with whom she associated." Gamble, "Reminiscences of Major John Grattan," 4. Catherine's character is also reflected in an incident recorded by historian C.E. May. Evidently a woman in the Shenandoah Valley attacked Catherine's reputation with disastrous consequences for herself: "On March 19, 1777, Catherine sued Bridget Simpson for slandering her. The court appointed Felix Gilbert and James Henderson to arbitrate the matter. The arbitrators found Bridget guilty, she acknowledged that the charges she made against Catherine were false, and the court fined her 100 pounds sterling," 229.

2. PATRIOTS YOUNG AND OLD, 1774–1791

The Grattans' aversion to British monarchs and their conservative leaders began in Northern Ireland. Taxes on tea, paint, and paper in the colonies revived memories of past mistreatment. As relations deteriorated between the colonies and the government in London, Catherine and her father joined the colonists opposed to the Townshend Acts. John Grattan sympathized with the opposition. As one relative recalled, "In the contest between liberty and power, he, like most of his countrymen, took the side of the weak and the oppressed."[1] When the British government closed Boston Harbor after its famous Tea Party, residents of the Valley of Virginia offered help. According to numerous accounts, John Grattan "contributed...a portion of the two hundred barrels of flour which were sent by the people of Augusta County to the relief of the inhabitants of Boston when besieged by the British army."[2]

John Grattan joined a local convention held to address the crisis. The need to select delegates to the Second Virginia Convention in March 1775 led to an assembly of the property owners of Augusta County. As one relative recalled, John Grattan "was an actor in the meeting in Staunton" in 1775, when the people declared their determination to preserve American liberty.[3] The freeholders selected Thomas Lewis and Captain Samuel McDowell as delegates and drafted a set of instructions for them. To make the views of Valley residents clear, the instructions were published in the Williamsburg *Virginia Gazette* on March 16. According to the gathering in Staunton, the king's "title to the crown of Great Britain rested on no other foundation than the liberty, and happiness, of all his subjects." The journey to the New World and settlement on the frontier came at a genuine cost, growing out of a desire to "enjoy the free exercise of the right of conscience." Therefore, they resolved to protect their rights "with our lives and our fortunes." Leaders in the Shenandoah Valley vowed that they would not surrender "to any minister, to any parliament, or any body of men upon earth, by whom we are not represented, and in whose decisions therefore we have no voice."[4]

Such strong sentiments led to the passage of additional measures. John Grattan and the convention supported the production of military supplies and the development of industries that would make them. They also tried to strengthen the militia—a force it described as "the natural strength, and staple security, of a free government."[5] In the gravity of the situation, Valley residents asked for divine help. Therefore, their leaders in the Valley wanted a day set aside for prayer, prayer to keep "America happy, virtuous, and free."[6]

When combat began, the Grattans responded. Although John Grattan was "too old for soldiering," a grandchild recalled, "he did the work of …encouraging others to do so."[7] Men in the Shenandoah Valley normally served in the state's militia. This opened the door to shorter enlistment periods than in that of the Continental Army, and a greater likelihood of staying closer to home. Two notable exceptions included John Grattan Jr., the only family member of military age, and Catherine Grattan's boyfriend, Robert Gamble. These men did join the Continental Army, serving as far away as Georgia and New York.

The American Revolution affected the family in different ways. Always short of male laborers, the Grattans' ability to run their businesses was stretched thinner. John Grattan purchased three slaves at this time, and probably driven by a general scarcity of workers, then added to their number. The war also led to the creation of paper currency and unexpected business difficulties, as one relative recalled, even for the very savvy Elizabeth Grattan.

The old lady, smart as she was, made one trade still remembered freshly by the family. She was in Philadelphia during the revolutionary war, selling her stock of cattle for a stock of goods, when some trader offered her scrip or continental paper money, for cattle, at the rate of two dollars for one of coin. When she left home, the depreciation was but fifty per cent. The apparent profits were too large to be resisted. Paper was bought instead of goods. The lady speculator set for home, exulting in her financial shrewdness. Each day's travel lowered her anticipation of profit, until she reached home, when three dollars in scrip were worth only one in specie.[8]

This was evidently one of the few poor transactions ever made by Elizabeth Brown Grattan, and her husband responded sympathetically. "But an Irishman's heart is ever fuller of love for a woman than money. John Grattan removed the depression from his wife's feelings by impressing his love upon her lips."[9]

Although Elizabeth Brown Grattan supported the Revolution, she found herself unable to forgo one minor pleasure frowned upon by the patriots. A relative remembered, "The anti-tea resolutions of the patriot ladies of the Colonies disturbed her very much. She had acquired such a strong love for it, that she could not dispense with its use. So she discarded the tea-pot from the table, drew her tea in a pitcher, and drank it as usual, letting it pass for a decoction of medicinal herbs, then very much in use for various complaints."[10]

As the conflict continued, the Shenandoah Valley was protected by distance from the maneuvers of large British armies along the coast. The real threat to the Valley came from the Native American allies of the British. Beyond such concerns, the Grattans worried about the safety of Robert Gamble and John Grattan Jr. Knowing that Gamble fought in a series of battles in New York and New Jersey in 1776, 1777, and 1778 gave rise to strong emotions for Catherine. News traveled slowly, and any knowledge of combat typically preceded lists of casualties. Relief always followed worry, but soon became anxiety for the Grattans' eldest daughter, and her feelings were well founded. Robert, at one point, served in a Virginia regiment as captain under Col. Febiger. Leading a company of select men, Robert attacked a British garrison at Stony Point, New York. One historian described what happened: Robert and "his men entered the fort first; then after the capture, and while he was attending to securing the prisoners, a Lieut. Col. Fleury came up, and seeing the flag still flying, hauled it down, thrust it in his bosom, and gained great éclat [acclaim] by the act. Believing that the gallant action of his command should have been mentioned in [the official] report, Captain Gamble complained to General Washington."[11] The famous general admitted "the injustice" but appealed to the young man's patriotism, "saying that it [the omission] was of importance to prevent any discord or jealousy from arising among our troops."[12] Consequently, the battlefield honor went to another.

While Robert Gamble served in many major engagements, John Grattan Jr., on the other hand, eventually found himself on the sleepy southern frontier of Georgia. It was a place of relative quiet in the first years of the American Revolution, and the news from him was not initially anxiety provoking.

However, in the fall of 1778, the situation in Georgia changed dramatically when the British attacked and captured Savannah. In the wake of this victory, they launched attacks on nearby American bases.

One historian writes, "General Prevost led his army from St. Augustine and captured Sunbury with its garrison on January 10, 1779."[13]After this force arrived in Savannah, a successful attack on Augusta placed much of the colony under royal control. Family records state that John Grattan Jr. died in military service at Sunbury or Lunesburg, Georgia, in 1779.[14] The young lieutenant perished in Prevost's coastal maneuvers. This shocking news devastated Elizabeth and John Grattan—in a time when primogeniture still lived, the heir to Contentment, the farm, the stores, and the mill was dead. Just as suddenly, the future of their remaining son changed. A relative commented, "Robert Grattan, the youngest child of John Grattan, was the pet and indulged one. Everyone did some work in former times. When Robert was a boy, and...whilst the grain was hauled from the field, his mother had a counterpane [bedspread] stretched over him, to keep off the sun, whilst he scratched on the fiddle in the shade."[15] A child of ten, ill-trained to run the Grattan businesses, was now the heir apparent.

The tragedy of John's death must have made the old dispute between Catherine and her father seem petty. Catherine's beau Robert Gamble served, according to a relative, "under the immediate command of General Washington."[16] Her mother probably pointed out to her father that his position looked absurd—one ardent patriot to obstruct the happiness of two others. In any case, John Grattan relented. George Gilmer writes, "consent was at last given, and the young lovers married."[17] Yet this statement is not very accurate in one respect. They were not young. When Catherine married Robert in February 1779 she was almost 28 and he was about 26, already middle-aged by eighteenth century standards—not the young lovers they once were. Having been frustrated for years, once Catherine and her husband married, they immediately started their family. A relative adds that Gamble obtained "furloughs once in every two years. At each succeeding visit he found a prattling babe to add to the pleasure of his renewed visit."[18] Catherine and Robert Gamble would eventually have four children, sons John Grattan and Robert and daughters Elizabeth Washington and Agnes Sarah Bell Gamble.

Later in 1779 John Grattan Sr. received an unusual distinction; he was chosen as a representative to Virginia's House of Delegates. According to historian C. E. May, the justices of Rockingham County selected him and Silas Hart. This placed Grattan among the very first residents of his county to be appointed to Virginia's legislature, presiding in one of the most important legislative bodies in the colonies.[19]

When John Grattan arrived in Williamsburg, plans had already been laid to move the capitol to Richmond. This did not keep those opposed to this decision from making one last effort to block it. On Nov. 2, 1779, according to the House journal, "a motion was made, and the question being put," "to suspend the operation of the act for the removal of the seat of government."[20] The supporters of Williamsburg lost by five votes, 40 ayes to 45 nays. After this vote, the House turned to a motion to explore "the better regulation and discipline of the militia." Evidently, a majority of the members wanted this topic postponed until March 1780, defeating the measure by 42 ayes to 34 nays. Feelings remained very strong on this topic and it produced one of the few recorded roll call votes of the session. John Grattan and George Mason lost, casting their votes to improve military discipline.[21]

Military topics filled much of the legislative agenda. The House voted on salaries of commissioners to oversee a gun factory in Fredericksburg, to "complete and continue the state regiment of artillery," and "retain" ships in the Virginia navy. Among the vessels named were the *Thetis*, the brig *Jefferson*, the galleys *Accomac* and *Diligence*, and the boats *Liberty* and *Patriot*.[22] There were also petitions for aid for disabled soldiers and the families of those who had died in action. A committee of the House, for instance, supported a measure to help Jesse Witt. Witt had "contracted an illness which deprived him of the use of his left arm."[23] Funds in varying amounts were also allotted to the widows of men in the Continental service, including the wives of Charles Gregory, John Cameron, Peter Wilson, and John Avis. Coming upon the heels of his own son's death, these acts must have been all-too-fresh reminders to John Grattan of the cost of war.

While John Grattan was in Williamsburg, major events occurred in the American Revolution. On November 13, 1779, a newspaper reported that a combined French and Spanish fleet had blockaded a major British squadron. Then it added that "Captain [John] Paul Jones in a frigate of fifty guns" had sailed "on a cruise under the American flag."[24] No one in Williamsburg at that time knew about the now famous engagement between the *Bon Homme Richard* and the *Serapis* on September 23. In the fall of 1779, American general Benjamin Lincoln attempted to recapture Savannah. The evidence of failure appeared in Williamsburg, as the casualty reports indicated that there were 450 dead and wounded Americans. Specific names were not listed in the article, but it portrayed the scale of the disaster by rank. The exception to leaving the victims unnamed was the announcement of the death of a

European patriot: "The gallant Count [Casmir] Pulaski died at sea, on his return from Georgia, of his wounds; and on Thursday last his funeral rites were performed here, in a manner suitable to the rank and merits of that intrepid and much lamented officer."[25]

When John Grattan left Williamsburg, British armies were grinding their way northward through the colonies. In the spring of 1780, Charleston fell with the inept General Lincoln and his army. The outcome of the American Revolution remained in serious doubt. During John Grattan's stay in Williamsburg, the family mill, stores, and farm were all under the direction of his wife and daughters Agnes or "Nancy," and Margaret. Robert, the "fiddle player," was ten years old and the newly married Catherine was pregnant. A seat in the House of Delegates was an honor truly valued by John Grattan, but it was an honor he could little afford. Besides his remaining very aware of the burden his absence created for his wife and daughters, a grandson mentions that he eventually became quite deaf.[26] At this point the process had already begun, and it was difficult for John Grattan to follow the debates.

Having reached a pinnacle of political and economic power, John Grattan began withdrawing from public service. Well into his fifties, if not older, he had outlived most of the men of his generation. With this in mind, and realizing that he had achieved most of his worldly dreams, politics no longer held much attraction. The American dream, the fulfillment of his ambitions, was no longer distant but at hand. With a degree of wisdom that age sometimes produces, John and Elizabeth Grattan chose to enjoy the bounty with which they had been blessed. The youthful ambitions of 1760 gave way to the Grattans' "contentment" during the 1780s.

News of the great victory at Yorktown in 1781 led to celebrations in the Shenandoah Valley. Some celebrated with food and drink, while others expressed their joy through faith. Given the sentiments of the Grattans, the older generation may have stressed the importance of church while their adult children expressed their delight in worldly ways.

The ending of the American Revolution brought Catherine's husband Robert Gamble home. When he inherited a farm in Augusta County in the 1780s, he and Catherine sold it. The capital from this transaction and funds from John Grattan allowed them to open a store in Staunton under the name "Gamble and Grattan."[27] The success of this venture depended, as did the early store at Contentment, upon Catherine's use of German. As her son put it, such knowledge "contributed greatly to aid my father when he commenced his merchant life..."[28] The new store also provided a place for Robert to begin learning how to run a business. John Grattan probably believed that the Gambles might have better luck at teaching Robert than would leaving him under the tutelage of his mother. And by the end of the 1780s, Robert had become a partner with his sister and her spouse.

In the Staunton store, Catherine was obviously an important figure, but so too was her husband. Robert Gamble had a genuine affinity for the mercantile trade. A relative noted that "his sound sense" found "constant application" in his work. To this, he added "integrity and aptness at securing the confidence of those with whom he dealt."[29] As the business grew, so did opportunities in other places. Richmond had less than 5,000 residents, but obviously was going to grow faster than Staunton. Realizing the possibilities, the Gambles decided to leave. At the same time, Robert Grattan's interest in the military led him away from the stores. Besides, his generous use of money conflicted with the Gambles' desire to reinvest in their business. In 1792, the Gambles and Robert Grattan dissolved their business relationship.[30] The family closed the store in Staunton.

These business decisions followed changes within the family. In the middle of the 1780s, Elizabeth Brown Grattan died. As she had always been warmer and more affectionate than her husband, her death was a real loss to her family. Yet by living into her mid-fifties she had outlived the average colonial woman by several decades. Without her presence, family history repeated itself. Daughters Agnes ("Nancy") and Margaret asked permission to marry, and their father initially refused. The reason he denied Nancy permission is not clear. Whatever went on with Nancy, she was remembered as John Grattan's most attractive daughter. Her nephew wrote, "My memory attests [to] her beauty, and I well remember when a mere child of hearing her pronounced the 'Beauty of the Valley' by young men who were the beaus of Staunton. She was beautiful in form as well as in the face, and when I saw her in Kentucky, 32 years after her removal from Virginia, I found her just such a person as my early remembrance of her beauty led me to expect to see."[31] In any case John Grattan did relent, and Nancy married Elijah Poage on July 31, 1787. The couple moved west and "settled within a mile or two of Lexington."[32]

Nancy's sister, Margaret Law Grattan, had a different fate. When she fell in love with Samuel Miller of Miller's Iron Works, Miller's father and John Grattan were bitter enemies. Unhappy with Margaret's choice, the old man refused to grant permission. Her nephew recalled, "Her father could urge no objection to her lover but that he was the son of a man towards whom he felt strong antipathy." Margaret countered with the notion that she "did not wish to marry the hated father." She rejected her father's logic, "finding the old gentleman obstinate."[33] Having observed much of the struggle between Catherine and her father, Margaret did not intend to follow in her sister's footsteps. A relative recorded her response, that when Samuel Miller came to visit "she leaped into the saddle and away [they went] to the Parson. The result justified her decision. Mr. Miller made an excellent husband, and they were a happy couple."[34]

Margaret seems to have been daring. Or as yet another relative observed, "Mrs. Miller was an open-hearted, free-spoken, fearless woman. When her husband was about fighting a pitched battle, soon after their marriage, according to the customs among neighbors at the time, she advised him not to strike too high, saying that a blow in the face might disfigure, but one about the short ribs would shorten the combat."[35]

Margaret was also as wily as her father, for she and Samuel Miller delayed their trip to the parson until John Grattan finished his will. When John Grattan wrote his will on November 23, 1791, he was still hoping she would marry a man of his choice or those of his executors. He offered her, according to one historian, "his best feather bed and bed clothes, her saddle, her clothes, a riding horse valued at twenty pounds sterling, 400 pounds sterling in silver, and a [slave]."[36] By running away and marrying Miller when her father was too ill to change his will, Margaret could instead deal with Robert Gamble and her little brother. They probably gave her her inheritance, even though she had crossed her father. The couple was, in fact, married six days later on November 29, 1791. To his credit, in his will John Grattan also provided for the well-being of his mentally retarded daughter Jane.

John Grattan's will begins with a summary of his beliefs and hopes, a powerful statement of the tenets of his faith:

> In the name of God, Amen. I, John Grattan of Rockingham County, Virginia, being through the abundant mercy of goodness of God, though weak in body, yet of a sound and perfect understanding and memory, do constitute this my last will and testament and desire it to be received by all as such. …I render up my soul with comfort, humbly beseeching the most blessed and glorious trinity… One God, most holy, most merciful and

gracious to prepare me for the time of my dissolution and then to take me to himself. I give my body to the earth from which it was taken in full assurance of its resurrection from thence at the last day. As for my burial, I desire it may be decent, without pomp or state, at the discretion of my children.[37]

Before John Grattan's death, his youngest son also requested permission to marry. This gave rise to his last known act, recorded by one of his grandchildren:

You know the old gentleman was very deaf, and his walks about home never took him to such a distance as to be out of earshot. Why [Robert]...did not effect his object with his pen I know not, but so it was that he...contrived a deer hunt, in which the old man should join. ...John Grattan] was placed at the first stand on the river bank, and [Robert] next, some two or three hundred yards further up, and as the dogs had to be sent forward sometime before, their music was soon heard in the chase. It would have been outrageous for... [Robert] to quit his stand until all chance of the deer coming that way had been given up. A deer, a long way ahead of the dogs, went down the opposite side of the river and crossed at [John's] stand; he fired and missed, and [annoyed] at once set off for home, which gave him such a start that ...[Robert] did not overtake him until near enough for all at the house to hear him shout his request, and on his arrival was greeted by all with facsimiles of the question he had shouted.[38]

The exact date of John Grattan's death is not known. It probably occurred in 1792, and unfortunately the grave is no longer marked. He was buried at Contentment within a short distance from the future resting-places of his son and grandson. John Grattan left six surviving children: Catherine was embarked upon marriage and business with her beloved Robert Gamble, Elizabeth and Samuel Brown lived near Lewisburg in what is now West Virginia, Nancy had moved to the Kentucky area with her husband, and Margaret and Robert lived in the Shenandoah Valley with their handicapped sister. John Grattan's death signaled the end of an era, and historian C. E. May used it to note the close of the frontier in the Shenandoah Valley.[39]

One can say that John Grattan died a free man in a free country, one liberated from Great Britain. As a Presbyterian Elder, he could have identified with one of the famous parables of the New Testament. Like a faithful servant who had been entrusted with resources, John Grattan had risked boldly and won a genuine measure of wealth.[40] Besides possessing Contentment, and its hundreds of acres, mill, house, slaves, and store, he had also received compensation from the state government for the loss of his eldest son. This took the form of 2,666 acres of "bounty land" in Kentucky. Steeped in faith, John Grattan left adult children who had the resources and characters to be extraordinary. The coming chapters will share what Catherine Grattan Gamble and Robert Grattan did with their tangible and intangible inheritance.

Notes:

1. Gilmer, *Sketches of Some of the First Settlers of Upper Georgia*, 26.
2. Ibid., 27. Other writers support Gilmer's claim:
3. Gilmer, *Sketches*, 26.
4. Van Schreeven, *Revolutionary Virginia*, 299.
5. Ibid., 300.
6. Ibid.
7. Gilmer, *Sketches*, 27.
8. Ibid.
9. Ibid.
10. Ibid., 28.
11. Alexander Brown, *The Cabells and Their Kin*, 256.
12. Ibid.
13. Coleman, "Restored Colonial Georgia," 6.
14. Gilmer, *Sketches*, 31 and C.E. May,
15. Gilmer, *Sketches*, 31.
16. Ibid., 28.
17. Ibid.
18. Ibid.
19. C. E. May, see also the *Journals of the House of Delegates*, 1779, 4.
20. Ibid., 36.
21. Ibid., 38.
22. Ibid., 74.
23. Ibid., 59.
24. *Virginia Gazette*, November 13, 1779.
25. Ibid., Dec. 3, 1779.
26. Gamble, 4.
27. Robert Grattan Jr. writes of the period: My parents "married on 17th October 1793...and they continued to live in Staunton and carry on the mercantile business for four years in partnership with Col. Gamble during the time of his residence in Staunton." Grattan, "Manuscript," 2.
28. Ibid.
29. Gamble, "Reminiscences of Major John Grattan," 3.
30. Gilmer, 32.
31. Ibid., 3..
32. Gilmer, *Sketches*, 30.
33. Gamble, "Reminiscences of Major John Grattan."
34. Ibid.
35. Gamble, "Reminiscences of Major John Grattan," 4.
36. C. E. May, "The Grattans in Augusta and Rockingham Counties,"

37. Augusta County Will Book #8, 20-22.
38. Gamble, "Reminiscences of Major John Grattan," 4.
39. C. E. May states that John Grattan died in 1792. *Life Under Four Flags*, 229-233.
40. Matthew, Chapter 25, Verses 14-30.

3. Big Sister and Little Brother, 1792–1806

The family that John Grattan began in the 1750s had changed in its composition by the time of his death. Some of his children had moved away to Kentucky and what is now West Virginia; their lives had little to do with events in the Valley and life at Contentment. The same would be true among John Grattan's grandchildren, some of whom would spend decades in Florida.

Among the family that assembled for John Grattan's funeral were his adult children in the Shenandoah Valley and four grandchildren—the two sons and two daughters of the Gambles. The eldest, John Grattan Gamble, was about twelve, brother Robert Jr., was ten and sisters Agnes "Nancy" and Elizabeth were children of eight and seven. Their mother and father, now about forty, were establishing their business in Richmond and selling their property in Staunton. Catherine's brother Robert Grattan, meanwhile, had begun planning his own future. Both siblings would display great daring and perseverance in their lives.

Robert Grattan was eighteen years younger than his remarkable sister. Born in 1769 to a mother in middle age, his birth followed those of four consecutive daughters. At that time, his sisters were unmarried. His parents, not having grandchildren when he was born, evidently treated him as if he were one. John Grattan felt less inclined to be as strict as he had been with his older children, and Elizabeth Brown Grattan protected Robert on those occasions when her husband did choose to be harsh. Raising children in an environment saturated with ambition had given way to raising this child in an abundance of success. One of his nephews described Robert's frivolity: "I well remember when he came to live with my father in Staunton, and of his being considered the handsomest young man in town. He was full of life and gaiety, and could out-run, out-jump, or throw down any of his [peers], and was always ready for a wrestle or a foot race. He was leader in all the fun and frolic of the town, and its unrivalled beau, equally ready for a dance or a bear hunt, or indeed for anything which promised fun or adventure."[1] One of Robert's sons echoes, "My father...was a boy of quick active mind and of a temper exceedingly gay...." Beyond these traits, another relative, George Gilmer, also found him to be exceedingly "generous." Or, as he put it, "His house was open to every one. His kindness was ever pressing hard upon his means. He resided near the public road from Staunton to Winchester. For twenty years the stage never passed by his gate without some kind of refreshments being sent to the passengers, and to Bogget, the old crippled soldier of the Revolution, who owned and usually accompanied it."[2] This custom, by the way, gave rise to the practice of leaving the local mail at Contentment rather than at the dwellings that would become Mt. Crawford.

Robert Grattan was very different from his father, but he shared his characteristic of extraordinary leadership. George Gilmer described him as being "a fine commanding person, six feet high, gray hair when young, and dark bright eyes. His spirit of command was so natural and easy, that his children never thought of disobedience, his household reverenced and loved him without measure. He was devoted to his wife and as kind a father as ever lived."[3] The strength of his relationship with his children was evidently not an exaggeration, and he combined it with a magnetic personality. His son Robert recalled, "The great superiority of my father over all the men I have known was the absolute control he exercised over every one around."[4]

Even though Robert Grattan rejected his father's aloofness, he admired his older brother's decision to join the Continental Army. It is easy to imagine this child of six or seven being impressed with his brother in uniform. The news of John Grattan Jr.'s death in 1779 galvanized Robert's commitment to the military. When the American Revolution ended, though, he was still too young to serve. With few options, Robert joined a local militia cavalry unit as a teenager. With genuine leadership skills and a membership in a leading family, he became an obvious choice as an officer. Augusta County records note that he was recommended as a "captain of a company of cavalry" on March 23, 1793, and some months later he was listed among the officers who had "qualified." Three years later in 1796, he was promoted to major in a unit described as "a Battalion in a Regiment of Cavalry [assigned] to the 3rd Division of the militia."[5]

Robert's promotion to captain in 1793 preceded his marriage to Elizabeth Thornton Gilmer by a few months, from June to October.

He obviously had known the young woman for some time, since he had asked his father for permission to marry her a year earlier. Prominent families tended to intermarry, and the Gilmers owned a large farm, "Lethe," seven or eight miles down the river. Elizabeth's parents had moved to the Valley about 1760, as had the Grattans. Her father's brother, George, on the other hand, settled near Charlottesville at Pen Park. Both brothers, Peachy Ridgway Gilmer and George Gilmer, were the nephews of Dr. Thomas Walker—a man remembered, according to one historian, as Thomas "Jefferson's guardian."[6]

While Peachy was establishing his farm in the Shenandoah Valley, his brother pursed a career in medicine. George attended, a historian writes, "William and Mary College...and studied medicine under his uncle, the aforementioned Dr. Thomas Walker."[7] In time, George received a degree of fame that had "surpassed" his well-known uncle's. As a neighbor to Thomas Jefferson, George Gilmer of Pen Park had far more than just a professional relationship. Historian Richard Davis wrote, "He was friend...of Jefferson and Madison, and in 1774 represented his county in the House of Burgesses. He was called, in the double capacity to all the great manor houses."[8]

Robert and his new wife could never have imagined how both branches of the Gilmer family were to become intertwined with the Grattans. Their marriage commenced at "Lethe," the Gilmer estate in the Shenandoah Valley. As they returned to Staunton, Robert's comrades in arms came to greet the couple. As a nephew recalled, "I accompanied his troop of cavalry which went some eight or ten miles to meet their captain and escort his young bride to town. She was, in my eyes, the smallest woman I had ever seen."[9]

While the new couple celebrated, protests in western Pennsylvania had already begun. Events came to a head in 1794, culminating in the Whiskey Rebellion. Farmers led by David Bradford attacked government officials, disrupting postal services, and preventing the collection of taxes. The fairness of the taxes can easily be questioned, for they fell on rural people who had little access to hard currency. It is not surprising that thousands defied federal laws, which Alexander Hamilton and President Washington saw as a threat to the new federal government. In August 1794, the President issued a proclamation demanding that the insurgents disperse, and ordered the governors of Pennsylvania, New Jersey, Maryland, and Virginia to call up 13,000 militiamen. The governor of Virginia, Richard Henry "Light-Horse Harry" Lee, complied, and directed Robert Grattan to muster his cavalry unit.

Robert chose the Augusta Stone Church as an organizing point. Located at the north end of Augusta County, it faced the main road to Pennsylvania. As the soldiers arrived, they found a major church meeting underway, debating the merits of the rebellion. The Rev. William Graham was supporting the insurgents but Rev. Moses Hoge wanted the group to endorse Washington's proclamation. As Robert and his friends watched, Rev. Graham, as one historian put it, "boldly avowed that the 'whiskey boys,' as they were usually called, were not rebels, but a suffering people, whose grievances ought to be redressed." Graham gained support from church members "who sympathized with the whiskey boys—whiskey being at that time a chief staple of the valley, and the tax upon its manufacture was felt as a grievance."[10] As the soldiers listened, their concerns went in a very different direction. *What about the violations of federal law? What about attacks on government officials? What would become of a country if people refused to obey an elected government?* To their amazement, Graham's position narrowly won, and Robert's men lost their patience. As the historian continued, "The soldiers were exasperated against Mr. Graham and his party, and threatened violence against him."[11] Without further debate Graham fled the church and the tumult.

Robert's unit joined the army organized in Carlisle, Pennsylvania. In addition, President Washington, Secretary of the Treasury Hamilton, and Governor Lee of Virginia arrived in uniform. The presence of such legendary leaders gave Robert Grattan memories for a lifetime. Of these people, a nephew recalled, General Washington "made the strongest impression."[12] At the same time, Robert's leadership of one of Virginia's finest units, a "splendid company of cavalry" as a relative remembered, also attracted the attention of authorities.[13]

Robert Grattan often reminisced about an event that took place during the Whiskey Rebellion: "[It was about] a bet made by Harry Lee, the most impudent of men." The governor of Virginia wagered with his officers that "he could tap General Washington on the shoulder, look him in the face, and ask him an impertinent question." Evidently, there was no shortage of men who believed that Lee was not that bold. "General Lee went up to the side of General Washington, then standing on the parade ground directing the movements of the army, and placed his hand familiarly on the general's arm." Lee's courage, however, quickly evaporated. "The great chief turned upon him his stern commanding look, until Lee shrunk away." Then Robert Grattan noted that the bets were paid, observing that these were "the only kind of debts he ever paid."[14]

Once troops crossed the Alleghenies, resistance by the whiskey boys melted. Some of the ringleaders were arrested, and David Bradford escaped down the Mississippi River. At the end of the rebellion, Harry Lee gave Robert Grattan his final orders. One of Robert's grandsons shared the letter:

Sir—As soon as you can make it convenient, after joining your troops, you will please to move by the way of Morgantown to Staunton...I prefer your taking a route to Morgantown...on the west side of the Monongahela River, if any can be found convenient. You will deposit your tents, & tc. [etc.], agreeably to general orders, at Winchester. The arms you will retain provided you hold yourself responsible to the United States for them. If so, favor me with a letter to this effect, enclosing a return of the arms.

I cannot conclude this letter without making my acknowledgments to you, your officers and soldiers in their cheerful and manly demeanor during the expedition. To me they have given great satisfaction; to themselves they have done great honor. I wish you and them a happy meeting with your friends, and shall always take pleasure in manifesting, by every means in my power, the high esteem I entertain of the merit of your troop. Sincerely, Rich'd Henry Lee.[15]

This letter became one of Robert Grattan's most treasured possessions.

The importance of the Whiskey Rebellion has been debated among historians. Since the opposition crumbled with the arrival of troops, it is easy to see it as a minor event. Historian Roger C. Kennedy, on the other hand, regarded it as having been a genuine threat to the Federal government. He described one of the whiskey boys who was tried: "John Mitchell was a bellicose brawler who had assembled with others, in arms, for the assault on Pittsburgh. He had joined in an attack upon a tax collector's house in which people were killed. He had robbed the mails to disrupt the government's communications. In each of these actions, he was seen by scores of people."[16] Such daring behavior encouraged protestors, who on one occasion numbered into the thousands. To add to the hostilities, the whiskey boys raised their own flag of six stars. Each represented counties, four rebellious ones in Pennsylvania and two in what is now West Virginia. Their leader, David

Bradford, according to one writer, "dreamed of himself as the George Washington of a new western republic."[17] Taking such a matter seriously, historian Kennedy writes: "Washington believed that the Union was in peril. His informed assessment was that 'the Western Settlers [stood] as it were upon a pivot—the touch of a feather would almost incline them any way."[18] The President's actions, then, removed the threat to the nation.

One of the consequences of the court cases that grew out of the Whiskey Rebellion was a judicial definition of treason. The prosecutor in Mitchell's trial stated that treason meant the "raising of a body of men to obtain, by intimidation or violence, the repeal of a law." This suggested the "levying of war" or the possibility of levying war. He went on to distinguish between talking about acting and actually taking action. This was an effort to separate peaceable assembly from an armed mob using violence and intimidation. In the trial, U.S. Supreme Court Justice William Paterson added a requirement that in order to convict one of treason, there must be at least "two persons" to witness the act.[19] In the early nineteenth century, this definition would become important in a different trial—Aaron Burr's. But that was still in the future.

In the following year, 1795, Elizabeth and Robert Grattan turned their attention to a major social event at her uncle George Gilmer's house at Pen Park near Charlottesville. On May 28th, the eldest of Elizabeth's cousins and a daughter of George Gilmer, Mildred, married a jovial author and attorney, William Wirt. Wirt would become nationally known for writing the *Letters of the British Spy* and a biography of Patrick Henry. Suddenly, within six months, the Gilmers were shocked by the death of Mildred's father on November 29, 1795; the family felt his loss immensely. As a historian recalled, "Dr. Gilmer was easily the most prominent physician in Albemarle County [Charlottesville] of his day."[20] William Wirt honored the doctor's many skills beyond medicine and said he was "a good linguist, a master of botany and of chemistry of his day— had a store of very correct general science—was a man of superior taste in the fine arts—and to crown the whole, had an elevated and a noble spirit and was in his manners and conversation a most accomplished gentleman."[21] In spite of their wealth of talent, the Gilmers of Pen Park were plagued with poor health. On Sept. 17, 1799, Mildred Gilmer Wirt, after only four years of marriage, died childless, leaving the author and attorney a widower. While these lamentable events weighed heavily on the Grattans, early deaths were an unpleasantly frequent aspect of eighteenth and nineteenth century life. Yet, tragedy opened the door to the unforeseen and unpredictable.

After the Gambles moved to Richmond and his father died, Robert Grattan closed the remaining store at Contentment. Having rid himself of the tedium of store-keeping, Robert felt free to live his own life. He turned to the law and received basic training in that field. Meanwhile, he and Elizabeth kept Contentment's mill and farm. Like so many of the Scotch-Irish, he had little use for idle country "squires" or the Tidewater gentry who lived, in his opinion, without working. A son recalled Robert Grattan's many responsibilities: "His family and friends and neighbors all trusted him implicitly. He was the Dr. and Lawyer and the peacemaker in his neighborhood. He wrote all the agreements and wills and did all the business that required writing in the neighborhood. He administered all the medicine, set the bones and did the bleeding. And I doubt whether there was a healthier or happier people in the world and one who spent less on Drs. or Lawyers, and the effects have continued even to this day." [22]

The difference between the gravity required for Robert's legal practice and his mirthful nature suggests the depth of his personality. One of his sons wrote, "And it is curious that whilst my father was living a gay light hearted and happy life, playing all sorts of games, dancing, singing, playing the fiddle, and having the gayest and most thoughtless men about him, he contrived to guard his boys with the greatest care from all the temptations of the world, and to surround them with the most healthy and correct sentiment." [23] Rather than celebrating such wisdom, many relatives preferred his passion for pleasure. A son wrote that Robert Grattan "...could lead the gravest to engage in gayeties that they themselves could not have believed they were capable. And when the mirth and merriment was at its wildest excess he seemed to hold it in his hand and control it. I have seen the oldest men and women that came to the house made to dance 'Father and Mother and I' until they would appear to be almost convulsed and they never appeared to suspect a Master spell was upon them." [24]

Robert's wife, Elizabeth Gilmer Grattan, was a full partner in his whimsical pastimes. One son wrote, "My mother possessed the capacities to amuse that is found in the whole family of Gilmers." [25] Yet she also maintained a degree of self-control that consequently "secured her the respect of every one." Elizabeth, a son continued, had many talents and little formal schooling. "My mother was a most acute observer and most independent thinker. She seemed to have an almost infallible judgment of character...without any education, scarcely, such were the powers of her mind and capacity to please that she was always the controlling lady in all companies."[26] The combination of these characteristics suggests that Elizabeth was well-suited for her husband. Loving and tolerant, she managed to add a degree of balance that he occasionally lacked.

The couple had eight children spread out over 17 years. Of these, two died before their second birthday. It was hard that the first to perish was their first child. Eliza Peachy Grattan, born in 1795, died a little over a year later in June 1796, most likely of a communicable disease. The couple was more fortunate with the next four children. Like other American families, the Grattans recycled the names of their deceased children.[27] When their second child was christened Elizabeth Frances Grattan, some dubbed her "Eliza." Still others called her "Bess," "Betsey," or "Betty." Her birth in April, 1797, preceded that of Robert Grattan Jr. in March, 1800, Peachy Ridgway's in November, 1801, and Lucy Gilmer Grattan's in Feb., 1804. The health of these children varied wildly, especially that of the two older sons. Robert Jr. recalled, "I have heard my mother say, that she had laid me down frequently never expecting to take me up alive. My brother Peachy was only about 18 months younger than myself, and he was of a robust constitution, and our Mother would put him down to scuffle for himself and nurse me."[28] Robert Jr.'s constant poor health left him smaller than most children. As he remembered, "By the time I was three years old Peachy was as stout as I was and we continued years after of very nearly the same size."[29]

Robert and Elizabeth Grattan were also challenged by the task of providing their children with a decent education—a challenge they both took very seriously, for the quality of local teachers left much to be desired. Robert Jr. described his experiences at length:

> The first teacher we went to was an old man by the name of McCoy, a tall genteel looking drunken old fellow. How much I learned I have no recollection. I have a distinct recollection of the Old Man's appearance with his long blue coat, coming half way down between his knees and ankles, with brass buttons. He carried a long cane, as high nearly as himself, and I recollect Peachy, who was left handed, commencing writing...at the wrong side of the paper. I recollect also a turning out of the Old Man by the boys. We all collected very early and barricaded the doors and windows. Presently the Old Man came and pretended to be...[angry], and...frightened all the little fellows very much but the older boys [however] maintained their courage and after

a while they pacified the old man by offering him a bottle of whiskey through a broken pain [sic] of glass in the window. He then demanded to know what we wanted, and we told him and he made us write down our demands and every one who could signed them. Those who could not write, made their mark to the demands, and the Old Man who I have no doubt was as much pleased all the time at being turned out, as we were at the prospect of holiday, consented to give us the time we demanded and we all sailed out in the highest glee.[30]

While Robert and Elizabeth focused on the education, health, and happiness of their new family, Catherine and Robert Gamble

Catherine Grattan Gamble

were establishing their business in Richmond. In an effort to reduce costs of imported goods, the Gambles invested directly in shipping ventures. As a relative put it, Robert "became one of the principal traders to Europe in the city."[31] He and Catherine were then able to stock their store with quality merchandise purchased at cheaper prices. Profits soared, of course, and they rapidly joined the ranks of the wealthy in Richmond. In 1799, recognizing that entertaining would further enhance business, they purchased the unfinished home of John Harvie. The house was spectacular, even "magnificent," as one writer in the twentieth century put it.[32] Harvie evidently knew the distinguished architect Benjamin Latrobe and used a set of his plans. Latrobe ultimately would be remembered for his design for the U.S. Capitol building. The Gamble's new dwelling stood on a hill overlooking the James River. It was, as the writer continued, "a big square house built of stone with a pillared portico facing toward the river far below."[33] Once the residence became their home, Robert named it "Grey Castle."[34]

As serious entrepreneurs, the Gambles set out to be a force within the community. Although Catherine Grattan Gamble had grown up on the frontier, she had been to Philadelphia on countless buying trips. Staying with prominent Scotch-Irish families, Catherine knew the genteel refinements

Robert Gamble

that appealed to professionals and the upper class. She now brought this wealth of knowledge to bear with her customary energy. One historian wrote, "Mrs. Gamble had the same zest for her role of home-maker as she had shown courage in meeting the dangers of the wilderness. Grey Castle became a home in which one found abundance, hospitality, dignity, culture, and love."[35] As the house became a social center in Richmond, the friends of the Gambles grew to include U.S. Chief Justice John Marshall, William Wirt, and various members of the Cabell family. Decades after Catherine's death, she was still remembered, according to one writer, as "one of the most sensible, pious, efficient women, who has ever influenced the society of the City of Richmond."[36]

Living in a city gave the Gambles attractive choices for the education of their children. As the Grattans struggled to find adequate teachers in rural Rockingham County, the Gambles found different avenues available to their children. A relative described the opportunities for the eldest of the Gamble children. "John [Grattan Gamble] was educated in the best schools of the county, and graduated at Princeton with the first honor of his class." This enabled him to serve in a unique position as a very young man. The relative added, "He was Chief Justice Marshall's Secretary, when he was the United States Minister at the Court of France."[37] At the same time, Catherine insisted that her daughters receive an education extraordinary for their gender. As one historian described the situation, "Elizabeth and her sister reaped the benefits of a national drive for improved women's education in the new American nation and attended a private female seminary under the direction of family friend, pastor, and local Schoolmaster, John Durburrow Blair. Parson Blair schooled his students in French and arithmetic, anticipating the curriculum of the Richmond Female Academy, which opened in 1807 and included classes in Latin, Greek, mathematics, history, geography, and natural philosophy."[38] Elizabeth's later success in running a plantation suggests that she and Nancy were also taught business skills, including bookkeeping. It is highly likely that Catherine made sure that these young women learned the financial skills her father taught her at Contentment.

While Catherine's sons followed their father into his business, her attractive daughters caught the eye of many gentlemen. Among the first to come courting was the widower William Wirt. The handsome and congenial lawyer was better known on the party circuit than he was among serious attorneys. Even though Elizabeth was seventeen and Wirt thirty, the youngest of the Gamble children evidently saw something in him that suggested merit. As one writer put it, "With a woman's intuition she saw good, even potential greatness, beneath the gay and apparently irresponsible exterior of the man who possessed wonderful talent."[39] While courting Elizabeth Gamble, Wirt gave reason for father Robert Gamble to have serious doubts. One of Wirt's nineteenth century biographers relates a telling story from the period:

> Col. Gamble had occasion, one summer morning, at sunrise, to visit his future son-in-law's office. It unluckily happened that Wirt had, the night before, brought some young friends there, and they had had a merry time of it, which had so beguiled the hours, that even now, at sunrise, they had not separated. The Colonel opened the door, little expecting to find any one there at that hour. His eyes fell upon the strangest group. There stood Wirt with the poker in his right hand, the sheet-iron blower fastened upon his left arm, which was thrust through the handle; on his head was a tin washbasin. As to the rest of his dress—it was hot weather, and the hero of this grotesque scene had dismissed as much of his trappings as comfort might be supposed to demand, substituting for them a light wrapper that greatly added to the theatrical effect. There he stood in this whimsical caparison, reciting, with an abundance of stage gesticulation, Falstaff's onset upon the thieves. His back was to the door. The opening of it drew all attention. We may imagine the queer look of the anxious probationer, as Col. Gamble, with a grave and mannerly silence, bowed and withdrew, closing the door behind him without the exchange of a word.[40]

During this time, William Wirt received an appointment as a "chancellor of Virginia." With such news, Robert and Catherine Gamble welcomed Elizabeth's marriage to Wirt. The Gambles entertained guests at a lavish wedding in 1802, creating quite an impression on Richmond society. Recalling the festivities, a historian described them as "a triumph of sumptuousness."[41] The guests included Catherine's brother, Robert, and sister-in-law, Elizabeth Grattan. The irony of the circumstances was undoubtedly not lost on this couple. Within a span of just over seven years, Robert and Elizabeth had first attended the wedding of her first cousin and then his niece: the bridegroom, on both occasions, being William Wirt. In early nineteenth century Virginia, though, it was a common occurrence for relatives to marry relatives. And it was equally common when one spouse died for the surviving partner to simply marry a different member of the spouse's family.

The relationship between William and Elizabeth Wirt differed from that of many early nineteenth-century couples. One historian states that Elizabeth "served as her husband's silent partner in both his law practice and in his commercial investments." She offered her views on legal fees, "supervised his law clerks, assisted with professional correspondence, and provided important business contacts."[42] In addition, Elizabeth exercised real control over the household. The same source developed a long list of her decisions that elucidates her unique position of power: "She bought and sold livestock, had the Wirts' land surveyed, contracted for labor on the family's homes, paid and refused to pay hired help, bought and sold slaves, hired and fired free white servants, and took a leading role in selecting and negotiating contracts for the Wirts' homes."[43] Many of these transactions were based on those of Elizabeth's very astute mother. Her mother, in turn, was very pleased with her daughter's economic and managerial prowess as both a woman and a granddaughter of John Grattan.

The atypical marriage of William and Elizabeth Wirt also apparently put an end to his prolonged adolescence. One account described the event as "a major turning point in his life."[44] From this point on, his practice of law and writing took on new urgency. In 1803, William Wirt published his *Letters of the British Spy* as a serial in a Richmond newspaper. Using the fiction of being a spy, he offered a lively and insightful commentary to Virginia and its leaders. The public responded with great enthusiasm and the book went through ten editions in less than 20 years.

William Wirt also began a series of legal positions—the first of which took the couple to Williamsburg. The town had been in decline since the capitol had been moved two decades earlier and it offered few financial opportunities for the aspiring attorney. Then in 1803, he gave up his governmental position to practice law in Norfolk. In this new location, Wirt added to the family's income by joining the seasonal court circuits, which took him away from home. Elizabeth often used these times without her husband as occasions to return to Grey Castle. The Gambles responded by helping the young couple financially and provided their first domestic servant—a slave.[45]

Robert Gamble encouraged the use of slaves in the household, and wrote William "to look out ...for [someone] for Betsy's chamber and a driver of her carriage and waiter—and if possible a good cook also—and I will endeavor to remit you ... or honor your drafts."[46] After these suggestions, the Wirts' staff rapidly grew to include five adult African-Americans and a number of children. It is also safe to assume that this had been Catherine and Robert's policy at Grey Castle. The practice begun by John Grattan had become well entrenched among his children and grandchildren.

Agnes "Nancy" Gamble Cabell

While the Wirts were preoccupied with their many endeavors, William H. Cabell was courting Elizabeth's older sister. "Nancy" Gamble's suitor shared many characteristics with William Wirt. Both men were almost the same age, both were attorneys, and both had been widowers.[47] Cabell's first wife had died of consumption in late 1801. At the time, he had already served in the state legislature for a few years, and he would come to be re-elected continuously in the new century. When William H. Cabell married Agnes "Nancy" Sarah Bell Gamble on March 11, 1805, he was already a prominent figure in state politics.

The marriage between Nancy and William H. proved very beneficial to the thirty-two-year-old politician's career. Cabell had already supported Thomas Jefferson as a presidential elector in both 1800 and 1804. His bride's family, Robert and Catherine Gamble, on the other hand, held many close connections to Federalists, including Chief Justice John Marshall.[48] Thus, when the state legislature convened in December 1805 to select a new governor, William H. Cabell was in a unique position to garner support from both parties. When the votes were cast, Cabell found himself elected Governor of Virginia. The margin of victory was very slim, just nine votes out of 189, but the Federalists had voted as a block.[49] Or as the Richmond *Enquirer* reported, "Of the 28 or 30 members who are said to constitute the

William H. Cabell

federal force of legislature, scarcely more than three voted for [William H. Cabell's opponent]."[50]

Cabell's mother-in-law, Catherine Grattan Gamble, rejoiced at the family's ability to influence state politics. She and her beloved Robert were the parents of talented daughters who had married men whose promise was being actualized. From their home, Grey Castle, the Gambles now had reached prominence beyond the great Valley of Virginia. Their relentless pursuit of the American dream had produced tangible results. The marriage of Nancy and William Cabell also brought the Grattans at Contentment back to Richmond. Robert and Elizabeth Grattan, the bride's uncle and aunt, joined the festivities and savored the remarkable good fortune of the Gambles. In 1806, the Grattans were beyond their mid-thirties and the older Gambles were in their mid-fifties. For the next few years, the family in the Valley of Virginia watched social and political events in Richmond with great interest.

Notes:

1. John G. Gamble, "Reminiscences of Major John Grattan," 4.
2. Gilmer, *Sketches of some of the First Settlers of Upper Georgia*, 32.
3. Ibid.
4. Grattan, "Manuscript of Major Robert Grattan Jr," 4.
5. Chalkley, *Chronicles of the Scotch-Irish Settlement*, Vol. 1, 272- 273, 285-286.
6. Davis, *Francis Walker Gilmer*, 4.
7. Ibid., 5.
8. Ibid.
9. John Gamble, "Reminiscences," 4.
10. Waddell, *Annals of Augusta County*, 206.
11. Ibid.
12. Gilmer, *Sketches*, 31.
13. Ibid.
14. Ibid.
15. Peyton, *History of Augusta County*, 327.
16. Kennedy, *Burr, Hamilton, and Jefferson*, 352.
17. Quoted by Kennedy, Ibid.,161-162.
18. Ibid., 163.
19. Ibid.
20. Davis, *Francis Walker Gilmer*, 5.
21. Ibid., 8.
22. Robert Grattan Jr.'s manuscript, 4.
23. Ibid., 3.
24. Ibid., 4.
25. Ibid., 5.
26. Ibid., 6.
27. Harriet Beecher Stowe, for instance, lost a child to cholera in Ohio. She later gave his name, Charles, to a younger offspring.
28. Grattan, "Manuscript," 6.
29. Ibid.
30. Ibid., 6-7.
31. Gilmer, *Sketches,* 29.
32. Palmer, "Gamble's Hill: A Rebirth of an Elegant Richmond," 1.
33. Ibid., 3.
34. The name also appears as Gray Castle. See Vera Palmer's "Gamble's Hill."
35. Ibid. 4.
36. Gilmer, *Sketches*, 29.
37. Ibid.
38. Jabour, "Quite a Woman of Business," 68.

39. Palmer, "Gamble's Hill: A Rebirth of an Elegant Richmond," 4.

40. John P. Kennedy, *Memoirs of the Life of William Wirt*, 91.

41. Palmer, "Gamble's Hill: A Rebirth of an Elegant Richmond," 4.

42. Jabour, "Quite a Woman of Business," 67.

43. Ibid.

44. See the *Dictionary of American Biography*, Vol. 22, 419.

45. Jabour, *Marriage in the Early Republic*, 29-32.

46. Quoted by Anya Jabour, Ibid., 32.

47. Compare the *Dictionary of American Biography* to Alexander Brown's *The Cabells and their Kin*, 249-250.

48. Palmer, "Gamble's Hill: A Rebirth of an Elegant Richmond," 5.

49. Richmond *Enquirer*, Dec.10, 1805.

50. Ibid.

4. A Time of Trials: 1806–1828

Having helped William H. Cabell become the governor of Virginia, the Gambles and Grattans focused much of their attention upon him. The Cabell administration began in a troubled era associated with events of national importance. Conflict between Napoleon and the British raged in Europe and spread beyond the continent. Both world powers tried to disrupt trade between the United States and Europe. European navies harassed the American merchant marine, violating the rights of this nation, which was then neutral.

In 1806, William H. Cabell was carefully monitoring the production of arms for the state militia. Virginia had appropriated a sum of $40,000 for materials and the salaries of a staff of gunsmiths—a decision that pleased the Grattans and the Gambles. Although Cabell found the superintendent of the factory, Major John Clarke, to be both "ingenious" and "vigilant," funds were exhausted by October, 1806. The governor faced an unpleasant dilemma: he could close the factory, or attempt to keep it running on promises alone. The consequences of closing the factory were very clear. The workers "had been induced…to come to Virginia from remote parts of the union. It was conceived that, if [Virginia] failed to furnish them employment…they would have been compelled to seek it elsewhere."[1] Once the gunsmiths left Richmond, production might never resume. As an alternative, the governor suggested to the workers that they stay, on the condition of his promise to take the matter to the legislature as soon as it met in December. On the 6th of that month, in his address to the legislature, Cabell placed the finances of the arms factory among the first items on the agenda. The workers seem to have accepted this approach, since many of them held personal contracts with the state. The governor did not, as he put it, "hesitate a moment" in keeping them at work.[2]

Fulfilling his commitment to the gunsmiths, Cabell moved to another concern: the situation at the new state penitentiary. According to the governor, 283 convicts were sent to prison, "153 had been discharged, five had escaped, 14 had died, and there now are 112 in confinement."[3] The governor hoped that this institution would fulfill its objectives, observing "the number of crimes has not increased since its establishment." The purpose of the penitentiary, he noted, was to prevent criminal activity "by the reform of offenders, and by deterring others."[4]

Governor Cabell then cautioned the legislature about expenditures on prisons. As he put it, "the liberal and humane policy of the legislature" led to a vast sum being spent to build the penitentiary. It had cost $135,000 and required more than $6,500 in annual expenses. Cabell questioned the wisdom of such spending. "Shall we expend so much money in the uncertain hope of preventing crimes by a system of punishment, and shall we give nothing to the establishment or support of a system of education, which would prevent them more effectively by inspiring a love of virtue?" The governor added, "Shall we expend so much in the efforts to reform Malefactors, and shall we give nothing to increase, to the virtuous poor, the facility of education?"[5] Cabell reiterated his message, "I admire...[the penitentiary] as an excellent system for the reformation of offenders. But I more admire a system for the general diffusion of knowledge, because it will more effectively prevent crimes, and produce other most substantial benefits."[6]

Other family members shared the value William H. Cabell placed upon education. The Cabells would come to be significant actors in the birth and the development of the University of Virginia, but that was still years in the future. More immediate concerns for the governor, however, came from the need for military preparedness. The undeclared war between the United States and Britain flared along the Atlantic coast. Perhaps the most alarming international incident occurred in June 1807, when the British warship *Leopard* fired broadsides at the ill-prepared American frigate *Chesapeake*. The latter ship had just left the port of Norfolk, sailing out of Hampton Roads without any thought of combat. After suffering damage, the *Chesapeake* struck its colors. British officers then searched the ship, removing four sailors said to be British. Of the men taken, three were Americans. This incident inflamed the American public, further straining already fragile relations with the United Kingdom. President Thomas Jefferson responded to this situation with an embargo against trade with the belligerents, hoping to force them to leave American shipping alone. The economic burden of Jefferson's Embargo Act of 1807 fell heaviest upon families engaging in international trade, and so, in Richmond, it penalized the Gambles, undermining their shipping with Great Britain and depriving their store of imported merchandise. The impact was somewhat softened by Catherine and Robert's business practices, which a relative labeled as "frugal," and by their many investments in real estate.

As Federalists, the Gambles were opposed to Jefferson even before his odious embargo. It is not surprising, then, that Catherine Grattan Gamble and her husband entertained Aaron Burr on a visit to Richmond when he was still Vice President. Having made her own assessment of Burr, Catherine would watch him subjected to a withering attack in the local press. Legal action against Burr, for he would be tried for treason, was foreshadowed by one of the city's newspapers, the *Enquirer*. On October 7, it stated that Burr would attempt "to sever the western states from the Union, connect them with Louisiana, and form the whole into a distinct empire."[7] Almost a month later, on November 5th, the *Enquirer* reprinted an article from the Philadelphia *Aurora* suggesting that Burr had "some sinister objective."[8] His goal, the paper clarified was to occupy Spanish land in Mississippi. Another article six days later named Burr as a participant in a "nefarious plot."[9] On Dec. 5, the *Enquirer* warned readers that Burr was organizing provisions for an army with a goal of seizing Spanish territory in Mexico.

Catherine Gamble no doubt read Jefferson's response. The President, issuing a proclamation on November 27, 1806, stating that "citizens of the United States are conspiring and confederating together to [attack] the dominions of Spain, against which nation war has not been declared by the constitutional authority of the U.S." In preparing for this "criminal enterprise," they are "fitting out and arming vessels," "collecting provisions," and "arming themselves." Jefferson warned citizens not to be taken in and "seduced" by the conspirators, stating that they would "incur prosecution with all the rigors of the law." He also instructed government officials and agents to be vigilant in performing their duties. The President concluded the document with the following order: "I require all good men and faithful citizens, and others within the U.S. to be aiding and assisting in the discovery, apprehension, and bringing to justice, of all such offenders, and in the giving of information against them to the proper authorities."[10]

Catherine then watched the *Enquirer* outline the charges against Aaron Burr on Dec. 11, 1806:

The scheme of empire was more comprehensive, than any man not well informed can conceive—but it is demonstrable, that is, the editor of this paper can demonstrate beyond a shadow of a doubt that the design conceived and intended by Mr. Burr, extended to:

- The establishment of a despotic government on the shores of the Gulph [sic.] of Mexico.
- That Mr. Burr was to be the despot.
- That from among his friends in the United States were to be selected, the materials of [a new nobility].
- That among his designs of empire were fundamentally predetermined, a formidable military and naval establishment, and that it was to be reared from the materials of the United States, combined with other foreign materials.
- That, of course, the seacoast, on an extensive line, was to be seized and occupied.
- That offers of honor and emolument were to be held forth to adventurers, and to every description of persons from all parts of the world.

This vast and dazzling project was communicated to very few—but we know to whom it was communicated—we can prove it, if the great culprit should be brought to the bar of national justice. The readers of this paper know we have never hazarded a declaration of this nature, without assurance doubly sure: the executive of the union is fully possessed of the facts.[11]

While Catherine and Robert Gamble worried about Aaron Burr, the *Enquirer* continued its coverage by publishing a letter from a "Gentleman in Lexington, Kentucky" on March 17, 1807. According to this document, Aaron Burr had surrendered to government officials at Louisiana. Before this happened, he had "swindled the merchants here out of about $50,000 and those in other parts of the Western country out of about $150,000."[12] Since the government's charges were becoming known, public anger was on the rise. The "gentleman" believed that if Burr returned to the region, he would "be treated to a coat of tar and feathers." Then he went on to add that all honest men should "drag this traitor and stupendous robber to the punishment he so preeminently deserves."[13]

Since Burr's purported crimes occurred in the far reaches of Virginia, the former Vice President was brought to Richmond. On March 31, 1807, the *Enquirer* proclaimed that he was "now in the city; guarded as a state prisoner."[14] Then it offered an account of his arrest from early March and the subsequent journey across many hundreds of miles. The newspaper explained that since the "overt act of treason...was most probably committed at Blennerhasset's Island, in the river Ohio, and within the limits of Virginia. [Therefore] his crime there will fall within the jurisdiction of the Federal District Court of this state."[15] Noting that the trial would occur under the supervision of the Chief Justice of the United States, the *Enquirer* went on to predict that it would "be one of the most impressive spectacles which any city in the United States ever witnessed." Aaron Burr, according to the *Enquirer*, had combined high public office and crimes that were among "the foulest and most atrocious that can possibly disgrace the inhabitant of a free country."[16]

Catherine Gamble watched a horde of Americans flood the city to see Burr's trial; the population of Richmond doubled. Following months of courtroom maneuvers, a grand jury was convened and evidence presented. Aaron Burr was indicted for treason and for the misdemeanor of attempting to attack the possessions of another country. To the shock of many, including the staff of the *Enquirer*, Chief Justice John Marshall extended to Aaron Burr a chance to obtain bail.

At last, Catherine and Robert Gamble could act. She sent their son, John Grattan Gamble, to join a small group of men with the funds to bail the former Vice President out of prison. For these efforts, the Gambles became a target of the *Enquirer*. On April 15, 1807, the newspaper stated that Burr had the "deepest sympathies" of the Federalists. Then it added, "No one can doubt that Mr. T. Taylor is a firm federalist. No one can doubt misters John G. Gamble and Henry Heth." These persons and others, according to the *Enquirer*, acted out their "decided opposition to the administration" of Thomas Jefferson.[17]

Such statements were an oversimplification. Aaron Burr had visited Richmond on a number of occasions and his friends held serious doubts about the veracity of the *Enquirer's* stories. Perhaps the last person to stampede to judgment was Catherine Grattan Gamble. Having taken her own measure of the former Vice President, she daringly defied public opinion. A local historian recorded Catherine's actions: "While Burr and Blennerhassett [one of Burr's associates] were out on bail they were wined and dined like distinguished guests. Blennerhassett kept a diary in which he gossips genially of Richmond people, and of kindness he received from them, in prison and out of it." Then, he added, "Mrs. Robert Gamble, mother-in-law of William Wirt, took him [Blennerhassett] under her wing [just as she did Burr]. Her home...was not far from the penitentiary, and she, sent delicacies to supplement the prison fare. When the heat of the dog days was at its height, 'a present of fruit and good butter and fine calves' feet jelly was sent, in ice, by Mrs. Gamble.' When free, on bail, [they] 'drank tea' at the Gamble Mansion."[18]

When the trial began, it was an excellent opportunity for dynamic lawyers with forensic abilities to display their talents. In his mid-thirties, with curly golden locks, William Wirt made a name for himself as one of Burr's prosecutors. He was widely acclaimed for his efforts to have Burr imprisoned.

In spite of the forensics, the government's case began to unravel. The chief witness for the prosecution was the commander of Federal troops in the West, General James Wilkinson, and he proved unconvincing. His testimony to the grand jury was so poor that it came within two votes of indicting him.[19] Events would have become explosive had the nature of the general's communication with Spanish authorities been known in Richmond during Burr's trial. As one authority writes, "Wilkinson had urged the Spaniards to have Lewis and Clark massacred and also recommended the assassination of old Daniel Boone, who was then settling himself in Missouri."[20] To muddy the water even more, one of the primary documents used by the prosecution, a letter, had been altered.

On August 20, 1807, after the government had presented a weak case, the defense moved that there had been "no overt act" of treason and none had been proven. At this point, the Whiskey Rebellion then came back to haunt the prosecutors. The earlier case required two witnesses. Who actually saw Burr commit treason? What were his acts of violence? If there were none, when did he threaten government agents with violence? Historian Roger G. Kennedy writes, "Comparing the 'circumstance' of the Whiskey Rebels 'to Burr's case,' wrote the Chief Justice, 'the prisoner at the bar was neither legally nor actually present at Blennerhasset's island and the overt act laid in this indictment cannot be proved.'"[21] John Marshall then declared that he would not emulate an English justice who used legal fiction to execute the innocent.

The case against Aaron Burr suggests two possibilities. If he intended to commit treason, the government had apprehended him and his associates too early. The acts of violence or the threats of violence had not yet occurred. If treason were in the offing, then waiting would have provided genuine evidence. The other possibility is Burr was not planning treason at all. If the government had waited, that would have become clear. Yet this may not have served Thomas Jefferson's needs. Historian Roger Kennedy believes that the president wanted his old rival permanently destroyed. A trial did not prove Burr's guilt, but it did ruin what was left of his reputation. In achieving that end, newspapers such as the *Enquirer* had done their duty well. Aaron Burr was as good as dead. Yet, with a mind of her own, Catherine Grattan Gamble rejoiced in her independent stance on Burr.

In October 1807, in the shadow of the courtroom proceedings was a more private loss—the death of Nancy and William H. Cabell's first child, Catherine Ann. Named for her grandmother, the infant daughter of the First Lady and the Governor may have died of a childhood illness—so very common in the period. The Cabells went on have to have seven more children, six of whom lived to have children of their own.

As his service as governor came to an end, William H. Cabell used his connections in the legislature to be selected as a state appeals court judge—the forerunner of the state supreme court. For much of the rest of his long life, he served Virginia in this capacity. As years passed, Nancy and William could not afford a separate residence. So, they lived with the Gambles at Grey Castle. Though compatible, William and Nancy parted along denominational lines. One topic of contention between the couple took decades to resolve—the issue of religious faith. William H. Cabell belonged to the Episcopal Church while his wife Nancy sided with her Presbyterian Scotch-Irish ancestors. For decades, William used the topic to avoid attending church. As the years passed, he eventually made the mistake of saying to Nancy: " You know I don't consider yours the true faith. Now, if you will join my church, The Church, I will always go with you." Nancy is said to have just smiled. Then came the Sunday when she said, "Now, husband, you must go with me to church today. I have united myself with the Episcopal Church, your church, and have taken a pew for us.'" William, from this point onward, had little choice but to attend.[22]

In 1810, the Gambles and Grattans were shocked by tragedy that befell Robert Gamble, Catherine's beloved. As William Wirt explained, "You will no doubt have seen, in the public papers, the loss we have suffered in the premature death of my wife's father, Col. Robert Gamble. In the full enjoyment of health and strength, of uncommon mental and corporeal vigor, in the active and prosperous pursuit of his business... he was suddenly killed, on the morning of the 12th instantly, by a fall from his horse. He was a faithful soldier of the revolution, a sincere and zealous Christian, one of the best of fathers, and [most] honest of men."[23] Robert Gamble had purchased a newspaper and was glancing at it as he rode on a street in Richmond. Neither he nor his animal saw buffalo skins being thrown from the top of a warehouse. The terrified horse bolted, and Gamble received a lethal concussion.

News of the death brought Robert and Elizabeth Grattan to Richmond. From 1806 until 1810, they lived quietly at Contentment. Their family had grown: Lucy was born a few years earlier in Feb., 1804, John in 1807, Mary Peachy in 1809, and, since one child, John, had died as an infant, yet another infant was named John Grattan, born in 1812. Beyond the time spent with his family, Robert divided his efforts between legal affairs and milling. As years passed, farming became less of a priority, and it may have been left to slaves.

The routine of the Grattans' lives was interrupted by visits from relatives. In 1809, a young and very ill nephew from Georgia chose to recuperate in the Shenandoah Valley. Soon after the American Revolution, Elizabeth's older brother, Thomas Gilmer, purchased land near Athens, Georgia. His son George R. Gilmer struggled a lifetime with illness. To recuperate he came back to his ancestral home, Lethe. During his stay George Gilmer enjoyed the hospitality of the Grattans and established what would become their lifelong relationship.

Several years later, Francis Walker Gilmer, the youngest child of Elizabeth Gilmer Grattan's uncle at Pen Park, stopped at Contentment as he passed through the Valley. Years earlier Elizabeth and Robert had attended the wedding of Mildred Gilmer to William Wirt. Thus, it is not surprising that Mildred's youngest brother would stop at Contentment. Francis Walker Gilmer was well known beyond the Valley. A child of five when his father died, he was left in the care of Thomas Jefferson and William Wirt. "Indeed, Jefferson commented that since the death of the elder Gilmer, 'I have ever looked on Francis as a son.'"[24] With guidance from both Wirt and Jefferson, two extraordinary men, the young man's flair for scholarship blossomed, leading him to study at William and Mary. It is not surprising that Francis Walker Gilmer was one of the best-educated Americans in the early decades of the nineteenth century. Although he was plagued by poor health, like many of the Pen Park Gilmers, he undertook a major assignment for Thomas Jefferson—to recruit European faculty for the University of Virginia and to purchase books to form the nucleus of its library. As a gesture of his admiration and respect, Jefferson offered law professorates to Francis at the University on more than one occasion but only close to the end of his brief life did he finally accept.

Inspired by Jefferson and Wirt, Francis Walker Gilmer took an active interest in the education of his cousins Robert Grattan Jr. and

Peachy Ridgway Grattan. Robert later recalled,

> A cousin of my mother's, Mr. Francis Gilmer, one of the most talented as well as one of the most agreeable and best informed men I ever knew, came to my father's on his way to Clarksburg and after staying several days with my father and mother he persuaded my father to let me go with him to Clarksburg. We set off and were gone some ten days, and I have always considered this trip as the commencement of my intellectual improvement. He talked to me and made me talk, and by the time I got back my mind had been completely awakened and put into action. Mr. Gilmer was afterwards sent to Europe for the professors at the University, and he employed Long Hey Daughson, Boncastle and Batterman, and after his return he was himself appointed law professor, but never lectured himself, having been taken sick about the time the lectures should have commenced, and died that winter. I have always considered that his death was a great loss to the University. After our return to my father's, Mr. Gilmer wrote a course of reading for Peachy and myself.[25]

While the Grattans had the distinction of studying under Francis Walker Gilmer, Robert's later statements suggest this was related to intellectual development, not to legal practice.

While this opportunity came to Robert Jr. and Peachy, their parents had to make extraordinary provisions for the education of their eldest daughter, Eliza Frances. She was sent to Richmond to study at the well-known Richmond Female Academy. During this period, Eliza lived with the Wirts.[26] When George R. Gilmer came to recuperate in Virginia in 1809, he met her at their residence. From this meeting grew a relationship that developed through written correspondence. When Gilmer returned to the Commonwealth in 1821, he was seeking to clarify his feelings. As he put it, "I felt a great curiosity to see [Eliza]. I wanted to know whether we would fancy each other upon sight, as we had on paper."[27] While in Georgia, he served several terms in state's legislature and had just been elected as one of its representatives to Congress. In the same period, Eliza Frances Grattan completed her education and returned to Contentment.

The thirty-one-year-old legislator arrived in the Shenandoah Valley on a Sunday morning in October, 1821. Knowing the family tradition of attending the old Augusta Stone Church, George went directly to the church to find Eliza. As he wrote years later, "The doors were closed. I found the son of the sexton, and inquired if Major Grattan's family were there. He answered, yes. I opened the door but was unable to go into Major Grattan's pew, which was next to the door, and elevated above the seats in front. The owner of the next pew invited me in. I had no power to hear the sermon from my curiosity to see the inmates of the pew behind me. I could hear a stir among the Grattan children. Very soon a beautiful young lady descended from the pew, and went to the stove, pretending that she was cold. I saw that it was not Eliza. When the service was over, I found that Eliza was at my uncle George Gilmer's twenty miles off."[28]

Still in pursuit, Gilmer remembered, "The next morning, I went to "Lethe". As I opened the outer door, Eliza Grattan opened the door from the passage into the sitting room. [Before I knew it], my arm was around her waist, and I was pressing her lips; a position which I have been constantly taking ever since, and ever with renewed pleasure. Eliza Grattan and myself settled the matter most interesting to us in a very satisfactory way, agreeing that after the session of Congress was over, we would take each other, for better, for life."[29]

The relationship between Eliza and George R. Gilmer departed from many of the narrow conventional husband and wife roles. A Georgia newspaper claimed that Gilmer "had married his Virginia cousin, whom he loved dearly all of his life, and she helped him campaign." This source went on to add that Eliza was present even under difficult circumstances. "At one country house, they slept in the room with the farmer, [the farmer's] wife and sixteen children. Next morning, he asked for a towel. The farmer's wife tore the tail off the shirt of one of the little boys and handed it to him."[30] With a marriage that seems modern by even contemporary standards, they embarked together into decades of political strife.

While Eliza and George were returning to Lexington, Georgia, Eliza's older brothers, Robert Jr. and Peachy were beginning to establish their careers. Robert explored the possibilities that Richmond could offer, and he observed Catherine Grattan Gamble and her highly unusual relationships with men. He later wrote,

I remained with Aunt Gamble [from early January] till the first of the next March, in hopes of being able to get into some business. But the winter of 1820–21 was one of the greatest depressions ever experienced in this country, and I found it impossible to get into any business.... The time was not altogether thrown away, however, as John [Grattan] Gamble, who was living in part of Aunt Gamble's house taught me bookkeeping, and I had an opportunity of seeing something of City life. I had the company of Judge Cabell [William H. Cabell], who boarded that winter with Aunt Gamble. It was the winter that the crash came upon Judge Cabell, and John and Robert Gamble [Jr.] ...I have ever since viewed with admiration the conduct of all the parties in their misfortunes, Judge Cabell was as unruffled as if nothing had happened; John and Robert Gamble were as cheerful and buoyant and confident of their eventual success as if nothing had happened, and Aunt Gamble was the master spirit of the party. I was at many of the consultations about the arrangement of Judge Cabell's business, and Aunt Gamble was consulted as one of the wisest of the party. Indeed, I have never seen any female with the same powers of control as she had, and it was evinced in all their consultations... I have often ...[thought about] the energetic decision and commanding influence of Aunt Gamble.[31]

While Catherine Grattan Gamble was a fearless and insightful person, the years between the death of her husband and Robert Grattan Jr.'s visit had been very difficult for her family. From George R. Gilmer we know that Catherine's sons John G. and Robert Gamble Jr. suffered business losses with Jefferson's embargo against international commerce and again during the War of 1812. As the Georgian put it, "they lost most of their inherited wealth."[32] It seems that they had recovered only to fall back in desperate straits in the early 1820s. Having been damaged by international sanctions, both Gamble men began casting about to find new avenues for success. The answer they hit upon was land in Florida. Seeking financing for their venture, they went to Elizabeth and William Wirt. By persuading Wirt with a whirlwind of dreams about the South, they were able to obtain a loan of $10,000. A move to Tallahassee in 1827, however, did not stop the economic roller coaster. Robert Gamble Jr. continued to teeter between wealth and bankruptcy. One of his grandchildren observed that her father would save Robert Gamble Jr. from economic ruin on two more occasions.[33] The younger Gamble men lacked their father's frugality and their mother's business savvy. But both men had people to rescue them. By 1827, Robert Grattan would need to be rescued himself.

Catherine's fifty-four-year-old brother, Robert, had never been a business manager, and his resources were suddenly overwhelmed by an unexpected disaster—the destruction of the house at Contentment. Catherine's nephew described the family tragedy:

> This accident turned us all out of doors in the dead of winter; the fire having occurred about the first of January 1823.... I shall never forget the next day. My father was not at home at the time of the fire, he had gone on a visit to Gen. Porterfield, and a servant was immediately dispatched...When he was told that the house was burned, he inquired eagerly if all the family were safe, and then if the mill was burned, and when told that nothing but the house was lost, he appeared to be rather thankful that that was all the loss, then depressed at the loss, but returned home as fast as horse could carry him to make provision for the family. But Mother was not a person to sit down and cry over misfortunes, and before he could reach home, she had had the kitchen cleaned up and all the little furniture that was left put in [it]. By the time Father returned, she was ready to receive him as cheerfully as if nothing had happened.[34]

Without any insurance to compensate for the losses, Major Grattan built a new house at Contentment that stands to this day. Robert Sr. oversaw the construction of a large dwelling measuring 48 by 34 feet, with three floors of living space, each consisting of over 1,500 square feet. Given his proclivity for entertaining, he did not want a staircase to intrude on the space in the central hall. It was accordingly enclosed in a separate room next to the hall on the southeast side of the building. With a staircase off center, this left a small room on both floors unlike typical floor plans.

The house also included a number of extra features. On the exterior it appeared as a Federal dwelling with two windows balanced on each side of the front door and five windows on the second floor, aligned with those below and the entrance. Nineteenth-century guests would have noticed that the bricks in the entire structure were laid in Flemish bond rather than common bond. The walls were three bricks thick and the foundation was eight layers thick, approximately twenty-four inches wide. Four chimneys, two at each gable end, stood over fifty feet in height, serving eight fireplaces, and towered above the house. On the opposite sides distinctive brick cornices ran under each eve, connecting the gable ends.

The grand size of the house was matched by its height. With thirteen-foot ceilings on two floors and a foundation approximately a yard above the ground, the new house at Contentment was larger than many early nineteenth-century public buildings.

On the interior, the house had eight mantels, each of a different style. Added to rooms and the halls were chair rails and wide baseboards. All of the rooms were plastered, even the basement, which may have been used by servants. To accommodate dancing at Robert Grattan's parties, the central hall was equipped with a flush railing about seven feet above the floor, containing large metal hooks. The hooks permitted the Grattans to hang chairs out of the way—a custom they probably got from their German neighbors.

Robert Grattan Sr., as stated before, did not have the funds to build such a home. He then compounded the precarious state of his finances by buying an elaborate carriage in 1825—one the likes of which had not been seen in the Shenandoah Valley. When the Grattans rode in it to the Augusta Stone Church for the first time, the minister could not hold service because the vehicle held the entire congregation under its spell.[35] The pleasure the carriage produced for its owner was short-lived since the purchase signaled to Robert's creditors that he could no longer manage his finances. Without new loans, the desperate father turned to his older sons Robert Jr., then 26, and Peachy Ridgway Grattan, 25. Their first thought, to sell all the assets and pay the debts, eventually collapsed under the reality left by their father. Both young men discovered that the family assets were dwarfed by the debts. On January 9, 1827, Robert Grattan Sr. sold to his son Robert Grattan Jr. all of his earthly possessions—the mill, the farm Contentment, 333 acres in Ohio, and 17 slaves—all for one dollar.[36] This action transferred the assets and debts to the younger Robert Grattan while giving the creditors some hope that their loans would eventually be paid. Foreclosure would only have generated losses.

This event signaled a change in family leadership. Although several of John Grattan's children were still alive in 1828, that older generation was becoming less active. Catherine Grattan Gamble was in her late seventies and her brother Robert was almost 60. The extraordinary matriarch of the family, Catherine, died on Dec. 24, 1830. Her brother Robert would live until 1841. Yet, this was no blessing for him, since his financial losses were followed by a stroke. Having lived with paralysis for over a decade, he eventually died on Feb. 12th.[37]

Elizabeth Gamble Wirt

Despite the difficulties of her brother and sons, Catherine Grattan Gamble had reason to rejoice in the last decade of her life. Both William and Elizabeth Wirt flourished while Catherine successfully steered her own estate through economic depressions that overwhelmed many of the younger adults. William Wirt, having won fame for his speaking ability in the Burr case, continued a combination of writing and legal practice. In 1817, President Monroe appointed him as Attorney General of the United States—a post he held for a dozen years with, as one source put it, "great repute."[38]

His reputation was based on more than Wirt's forensic skills. One brief biographical account notes his managerial ability. "He was the first attorney general to organize the work of the office and to make a systematic practice of preserving his official opinions so that they might serve as precedents for his successors."[39] Beyond his public duties, William also maintained a prestigious private practice. Representing clients in one or the other of his capacities, he participated in a series of major cases—including one involving Dartmouth College. His combination of talent and skill helps to explain how William Wirt holds the extraordinary distinction of having kept a cabinet position for two terms under one president and then keeping it for four years under the next, John Quincy Adams.

William Wirt

William's wife, Elizabeth Gamble Wirt, continued to chart a life very different from other women. In 1829, she used her knowledge of botany and literature to write a book, *Flora's Dictionary.* This work was greeted with great success, so much so that one historian wrote, "the book proved so popular that numerous pirated copies were in circulation…even after the release of several enlarged editions."[40] In time, Elizabeth would drop the use of anonymity, a common practice for women authors, and the 1855 version of her popular book carries her name on the title page. The publisher, finding the work in demand, paid her $1,000 for the rights to a revised edition. The scale of Elizabeth Wirt's achievement is significant when you consider that an attorney described $800 as a "year's earnings" in the Shenandoah Valley in 1823.[41]

Catherine Grattan Gamble rejoiced at these successes and in her own. After her death, William H. Cabell described her estate: "Mrs. Gamble left a will, by which she gave to Agnes and to Mrs. Wirt all her furniture and everything about her house. She gave to John Gamble a lot in Richmond and a small piece of coal land in Chesterfield [County] both of which she had bought from him—all the rest of her estate is to be equally divided between her four children. Their part of her estate will amount to at least $36,000."[42] Given that her husband, Robert Gamble, had been dead for 20 years, this fortune reflected her own business and managerial prowess. Talent that she cultivated on the North River and in the Valley had led to immense success in Richmond. She had navigated the pitfalls of economic depression, those that destroyed the resources of her sons and one of her sons-in-law. In the world of finance, Catherine Grattan Gamble was as formidable as John Grattan. She, of all his children, was his true heir. The monument at Catherine's grave honors her exceptional nature:

> "There was no wife more devoted,
> No mother more affectionate,
> No friend more true,
> No neighbor more kind,
> No Christian more pious."[43]

Notes:

1. *Journal of the Senate of the Commonwealth of Virginia*, 1806, 7.
2. Ibid., 8.
3. Ibid., 9.
4. Ibid., 12.
5. Ibid.
6. Ibid.
7. Quoted in V.B. Reed and J.D. William's, *The Case of Aaron Burr*, 28.
8. Ibid., 36.
9. Ibid., 37.
10. Ibid., 42.
11. Ibid., 46.
12. Ibid., 84.
13. Ibid.
14. Richmond *Enquirer.*
15. Ibid.
16. Ibid.
17. Ibid.
18. Mary N. Stanard, *Richmond: Its People and Its Story*, 100.
19. "The general showed the jury the letter, but he was obliged to confess that he had tampered with it, scratching out a word here and there and substituting other words, erasing the entire first sentence. There were jurors who believed that he had written the whole thing in the first place, and that he was at least as guilty as Burr, possibly more so. To these it seemed patent that he was telling the story he told, hanging his former partner, purely and simply in order to save his own fat neck. These jurors would have indicted the General as well as Aaron Burr. ...When it came to a vote, there were seven grand jurors in favor of indicting Wilkinson, nine opposed." David B. Chidsey, *The Great Conspiracy: Aaron Burr and His Strange Doings in the West*, 118-119.
20. Roger G. Kennedy, *Burr, Hamilton, and Jefferson: A Study in Character*, 282.
21. Ibid., 352.
22. Alexander Brown, *The Cabells and Their Kin*, 255.
23. John P. Kennedy, *Memoirs of the Life of William Wirt*, Vol. 1, 285.
24. *National Cyclopaedia of American Biography*, Vol. XIX, 329
25. The professors hired by Gilmer were, in fact, George Blaetermann (modern languages), Thomas Hewett Key (mathematics), George Long (ancient languages), Robley Dunglison (medicine), and John Patton Emmet (science). Bryson, *Virginia Law Reporters before 1880*, 45. The quotation is from Grattan, 9-10.
26. Gilmer, *Sketches*, 275.
27. Ibid., 217.
28. Ibid., 218.

29. Ibid.

30. "Georgia Notebook," a column in an unknown newspaper, see the George R. Gilmer file at the Atlanta Historical Society.

31.   Grattan, "Manuscript of Major Robert Grattan Jr.," 13-14.

32. Gilmer, *Sketches*, 29.

33. Sarah Jane Gamble, "Reminiscences."

34. Grattan, "Manuscript of Major Robert Grattan Jr.," 16.

35. C. E. May, "The Grattans in Augusta and Rockingham Counties," 7.

36. *Burnt Deed Book 7*, Rockingham County, Virginia, 352.

37. His obituary described Robert Grattan, Sr; "He was intelligent, yet unassuming; firm and lion-hearted, yet gentle as the most unoffending; his heart sympathized with the whole world; he was the prince of hospitality. Who ever came to his door and he clothed him not, hungry and he gave him not food, houseless and he took him not in? As a neighbour he was ever ready to lend his assistance, and his services, though so often required, were always given with a zeal and kindness that enhanced the favour." *Rockingham Register*, Feb. 20, 1841.

38. *National Cyclopaedia of Biography*, Vol. Xl, 86.

39. *Dictionary of American Biography*, Vol. XXI.

40.   Jabour, "Quite a Woman of Business," 73.

41. Bryson, *The Virginia Law Reporters*, 44.

42. William H. Cabell to Henry Carrington Cabell, Jan. 5, 1831. Virginia Historical Society.

43. Burton, *Annals of Henrico Parish*, 450.

Contentment as the Grattans knew it.

5. A Scientific Farmer
1829–1850

The Grattan family produced a "person of distinction" in four consecutive generations. As the second generation died or grew to old age, leadership passed from John Grattan's children to his grandchildren. These family members, young adults on the North River, faced a crisis in 1827. A generation later, their children would face yet another. Before the Grattans could occupy a leadership role in the Valley on the eve of the Civil War, they would have to save their family farm. Robert Grattan Jr. purchased Contentment, then composed of 600 acres that included the family gristmill, the large new family house and seventeen slaves, all for one dollar. It was a poor business deal since his father's debts outweighed all of the assets. Moreover, the prospects of turning the situation around were not bright. Having been away in West Virginia establishing a legal career for more than a year, he was shocked at what he discovered on his return in the fall of 1826:

> I found everything in the most dilapidated condition. The [new] house had never had steps put to it, and the cellar was in one room. The barn had fallen to one side by the rotting of the under logs…. The fields were covered with briers and bushes, except where they were too poor to produce them. Some of them were gullied …[without a blade] of grass, except upon the ridges, between the gullies. The capital I had was not sufficient to have placed the property in good condition, much less to pay for it. The whole of the money was due, and what was worse, I was compelled to assume the weight of the debts.[1]

Sadly for Robert Jr., his account is not an exaggeration—for others confirm the bleak conditions he faced. George R. Gilmer recalled, "When he took charge of his father's plantation, it was overrun with briers and yielded but little profit."[2] The financial conditions were so poor that the deed itself includes the statement that Robert and Peachy were willing to sell the property to settle family debts.[3]

When Robert Jr. returned to Contentment in 1826, he held beliefs that made his tasks difficult. As he wrote, "I had commenced life with two resolutions, the one was to owe no man anything, and the other to have nothing to do with Negroes. And here I was compelled to take upon myself, an amount of debt, that has never been entirely removed, and which necessarily involved the management of slaves."[4] While his distaste for the institution of slavery matched his fear of debt, his father had bequeathed to him the very responsibilities he did not want.

From Robert's autobiography, it is easy to trace his lack of preparation for managing a farm. When he was a teenager, his father hoped he would become a merchant. The elder Grattan obtained a place for him as a helper in a store. Such aspirations unraveled in the economic depression at the beginning of the 1820s. This did not, however, keep Robert Jr. from wanting to add to his business skills. Consequently, he went to stay at Catherine Grattan Gamble's house in Richmond. This did not lead to opportunities there, but he did learn bookkeeping skills from one of Catherine's sons. Without reasonable business prospects, Robert Jr. turned to law and began studying under the tutelage of his uncle George Gilmer, the owner of "Lethe." Looking for broader opportunities, he went to Ohio in 1824. On the way back he visited his aunt and uncle, Elizabeth Grattan Brown and Sam Brown at Lewisburg, in what is now West Virginia. Robert wrote,

> [I] stopped at William Lewis's on South Mountain and he went with me to Col. Brown, near Lewisburg, where we stayed all night, and at their suggestion, I was induced to think of Lewisburg as a place of future location. I returned home and spent the winter and...in April 1825. I moved to Lewisburg and settled. It appeared to me then as it has turned out, that it was the most important point in western Virginia. When I went to Lewisburg there was but between three and four hundred persons in the town, and but four brick houses that I can now recollect. It [the town] then had, however, a Chancery court, under the old chancery system which made it a point of importance....[5]

His elderly relatives warmly received Robert.

Col. Brown, who married a sister of my father, lived about

two miles from Lewisburg, and with them an old Gentleman, by
the name of Grattan. He was a distant relation of my Grandfather,
and had lived [at Contentment] when he first came to the country.
He became greatly attached to my Father, and when I went out
to that country, he seemed to transfer his attachment from my
father to me. The three old people were each characters, and
primitive characters. They all treated me with great kindness,
and Charles Grattan who was an old bachelor and wealthy, about
the time my board became due, gave me a note [worth] … about
eight hundred dollars…afterwards, when he died he left me…
between two and three thousand dollars.[6]

In establishing his practice, Robert Grattan Jr. developed a
practical strategy, reflecting considerable wisdom:

My preparation for the practice of law had been of the poorest
kind. However, I used every exertion both by attendance on the
business of the court and diligent reading to remedy that defect,
and I have no doubt that the diligence I used would eventually
have made me capable of doing business. I made it a constant
rule to have a docket made out, and I marked on it every thing
that was done in every case, and I soon knew more about what
was the condition of every case in court, than any one of the
bars. The office of sheriff was [given]…to two young men who
boarded in the same house with me, and had their office next
door to mine. We soon became acquainted and I made myself
acquainted with the law appertaining to their business. By being
extremely cautious never to give them an opinion without being
certain I was right, I acquired their confidence. They soon began
to advise individuals that I was the most reliable person they
could consult. Although I made nothing scarcely…[while] I lived
in Lewisburg, the docket will show when I left there, that it was
a fair way to be compensated for all my labor and pains.[7]

While Robert Grattan Jr. established a law practice he would
give up, his brother struggled with the family's finances. On August 19,
1826, Peachy wrote, "My trials and my difficulties are pressing upon me
and I see no way to get free of them… all is so dark and gloomy around
us." A month later, he continued in despair, "…shadow clouds and the
darkness of the world's obstacles are thickening around me."[8]

In the fall of 1827, Robert Jr. and Peachy were forced to sell part of the family's personal property, paying the creditors something to buy time. In desperation, they sold the majority of their slaves, leaving the family estranged from their remaining servants. This tragedy befell seventeen individuals: "Henry, George, Harry, and Ben. Flora with her daughter Hannah, Servina with children Luvana, Malvania, and James. Lavina with her child Clara, Mary and her children Thorton, Cyrus, Robinson, and Agga."[9]

The significance of the sale was not lost on the Grattans, especially the patriarch. In the turmoil, Robert Grattan Sr. suffered a stroke. Still another tragedy awaited the family, Robert Jr. recalled,

...our sister Mary living in Harrisonburg, when father was taken ill, rode home in the rain, and exposed herself and over-exerted herself, for several days whilst my father lay at the point of death. The whole family [was so] absorbed by our Father's situation, that we did not perceive that extent of Mary's illness. Such was her energy and devotion, that before she...acknowledge [d] she was sick, she was at the point of death....She died on the 28 day of January 1828.[10]

Mary Grattan was only seventeen at the time. Her shocking death may explain her brother Peachy's observation from the period: I am "poor and needy and helpless. I am in the very dust, and there I must remain unless my Heavenly Father is pleased to raise me up."[11] Peachy's spiritual diary of the period is a running account of despair.

In this crisis, Robert Grattan Jr. received help and support from his mother and a younger sister. As he recalled, "I was encouraged and assisted, and enabled to get on by the devotion and self-denial of mother and Lucy. They enabled me to live upon little or nothing, and were ever ready to make any sacrifice of their engagements or comforts than I was to ask it. Harassed daily with some debt that I was compelled to provide for, and disappointed in my crops from the inability of the land to produce anything, I still enjoyed life from the affection and devotion of Mother, Father, and Lucy." They "revealed to me the true source of happiness: LOVE and DUTY."[12] Robert Grattan Jr. found himself with a mission. For the second time in its history, Contentment was in the grasp of an owner driven by very clear objectives. His grandfather, John Grattan, pursued a

Scotch-Irish version of the American Dream; Robert wanted to save the farm and the family's reputation. In the younger man's world, the priorities were quite different. For John Grattan farming was a minor priority behind milling, public service, and merchandizing. But without a store, Robert Grattan made the eroded, abused soil of Contentment a primary concern, trying to make every part of the Grattans' holdings productive.

Robert Grattan Jr. wanted flourishing crops, and he turned to others for the knowledge of how to achieve this end. He would later explain:

> I have always considered that the best farmers of Albemarle were ahead of any [other] part of Virginia, in the cultivation of their lands. When I first visited in Albemarle, the plowing was greatly better than it was in my own County, and my neighborhood are indebted to them for part of their improvement in that respect. When I first commenced farming, we all plowed with two horse plows and right about, up and down the hills. The first winter after I commenced farming, I learned from Hugh Minor to take advantage of the land in plowing, and that it was not necessary to plow land in twenty feet beds on hillsides."[13]

Yet with far fewer laborers than planters near Charlottesville, Robert Grattan could not adopt all of their techniques. "The great defect when I first visited in Albemarle, in their farming, was the waste of labor, they had always had though, laborers of their own, and no one thought of economizing it. They did many things with the hoe that might have been done much more economically with the plow and roller. They have improved as much in this respect, as we have in the plowing.[14] Robert borrowed the techniques of farmers across the Blue Ridge and adapted them to labor conditions in the Shenandoah Valley. He also bought clover and planted it extensively.

In the process of reforming the agricultural practices of the past, Robert Grattan Jr. made mistakes that he openly acknowledged. Yet he continued to learn and improve,

> Experience has modified many of my opinions, on the subject of farming, as on many other subjects. When I commenced farming my impression was that all that was important to land, was to fill it with vegetable matter, and I still think when the vegetable

matter has been exhausted out of the land, as completely as it was out of mine, that the first and most necessary improvement is to restore ...vegetable matter. My latter experience has induced me to think that lands of original good quality may be restored to its original fertility by being grazed judicially. It improves from two processes, one is from the excrement of the cattle, and the other from the fact that under a sod a certain amount of circulation is carried on, and by that means the various constituents necessary to the soil are brought up. The water that falls on the land in the form of rain and snow, is carried down and dissolves the various salts, and then, by the returning circulation, brings them up and they are combined with the various acids formed by the decomposing vegetable matter in the land.[15]

To carry out the restoration of soil at Contentment required time. This, combined with the many outstanding loans, meant that Robert had to economize for years. He later wrote,

The first four years of my farming life was little varied. I worked hard and lived low, and Mother and Lucy, by their self-denial, and economy enabled me to totter on under the load I had to carry. I verily believe that the happy cheerful manner, we all bore our privations, enabled me to sustain the load. Our cheerfulness gave confidence to every one, as men look upon cheerfulness as a symptom of success, and I believe they are right, for it certainly helps men to succeed.[16]

This steady lifestyle departed from the pattern of Robert's father and won the respect of the family's creditors.

His demeanor, presence of self, also earned him the respect of more affluent family members. Although he could have turned to Catherine Grattan Gamble for financial assistance and to his sister Eliza, the wife of Georgia congressman George R. Gilmer, it was not necessary, since he had the monetary backing of his uncle, George Gilmer, the owner of "Lethe." This third George Gilmer was the uncle of congressman and nephew of the Pen Park George Gilmer. Robert Grattan Jr. had a very warm relationship with him, so it is understandable that he turned to the older man.[17]

Robert Grattan Jr. also held assets that contributed to his economic survival. He was never limited to just farming for an income.

Within a year of his return to Rockingham County, he was appointed "justice of the peace"—a position he kept for decades even after the job became an elected position. In addition, the mill continued to be a source of revenue.

Social events and invitations, though not abundant, punctuated the Grattans' routine of frugal living. In 1828, Robert Jr. attended a wedding in Charlottesville. Here he met Martha "Patsy" Minor—the daughter of Lucy and Peter Minor. Lucy Gilmer Minor was one of the few Pen Park Gilmers to live a lengthy life and was the first cousin of Robert's own mother. Lucy was also a sibling of both Mildred Gilmer Wirt, the first wife of William Wirt, and of Francis Walker Gilmer, who had drafted a course of study for Robert Jr. more than a decade earlier. Also in Pen Park country, a major meeting was held in Charlottesville to focus upon the building of turnpikes and roads in state. By attending, Robert Grattan Jr. could both encourage developments valued by Shenandoah Valley residents and see Patsy. He later wrote,

> We [John B. Bolin and Col. McLaughlin] attended and were the only representatives from west of the [Blue Ridge] Mountains. I was delighted with the result of my patriotic exertions, for the welfare of the country. I had an opportunity, I never had had again, of seeing some of our most distinguished men. Mr. Madison, Mr. Monroe, Chief Justice Marshall, Mr. Johnson, Mr. Leigh, Judge Colater, Mr. James and Phillip Barbour, Mr. Rives, Gen. Breckenridge, Gen. Blackhoun, and many others. But what was more to my purpose, my cousin Patsy, was in Charlottesville also. [Then Robert made an observation], I came to the conclusion that there never had been a more distinguished set of men, brought together, for any purpose who knew so little about what they came for.[18]

Robert Grattan's financial crisis ended in the 1830s through a successful alliance and an inheritance. Robert Jr. courted Patsy Minor in 1828, only to be rejected. Over the next few years, they saw each other occasionally, and Robert continued his interest. He later came to see the wisdom in her first response, "I have always been thankful that she did reject me, it saved her from four years of great trial and discomfort."[19] Patsy did finally agree and they were married on the 9th of August 1832. Patsy's mother gave the couple a sizable monetary gift, which was always remembered thankfully by Robert Grattan Jr.:

[Because of my wife's] Mother, I was very much relieved of my [financial] embarrassments. I am under too many obligations to Patsy's Mother, for too many kindnesses, to pass her by, without a more extended notice. Cousin Lucy Minor had the Gilmer talent, for amusing in as high, if not higher degree, than any of the name. As Pen Park had been the center of all the society of the neighborhood, in the days of Peter Carr and Judge Carr and Mr. Wirt, so Ridgway [the Minor Estate] was the acknowledged focus of it, in our day. Cousin Lucy Minor was not only the most agreeable, but also one of the most sensible women I ever met. She was too good not to be wise, for wisdom comes of the heart, as often as of the head. So entirely unselfish and benevolent was she that her feelings always drew in the right direction. She was one of a very few persons, whose religion consisted more in piety than theology. I never heard her say an unkind or disparaging thing of any sect, or denomination. She was a low church Episcopalian, a class of Christians to which [belong] some of the best specimens of religious people I ever knew.[20]

Robert Grattan Jr. also received part of the estate of his Uncle George Gilmer of Lethe. This man was the bachelor brother of his mother and he divided his property between his three sisters. Since only Robert's mother had children, the shares given to the elderly women eventually went to Robert and his siblings. One of these aunts was blind, which forced her to move to Contentment, making the Grattan household even more difficult, since it still included the partially paralyzed Robert Grattan Sr. Or, as Robert put it, his home included "two old persons, who [are] sick and complaining, and often unreasonable."[21] Yet, Patsy Minor Grattan took such in stride. Robert recalled,

I could not but marvel at her thoughtful untiring kindness... I often felt ashamed of myself when I lacked in attentions to two persons, to whom I owned [sic] so much and loved so well, when I saw how thoughtful and good-tempered Patsy always was. It may be thought a small matter to treat kindly two old persons who were sick and afflicted, and so it would have been for a day, or a week or a month, but to hear their complaints, to administer to their wants, not only constantly, but kindly and never to forget or tire, and that for years, is a trial of temper and principle that few are capable of encountering successfully. One great act of heroism comes within the ability of many generous minds, but the performance of unobserved painful duties, for many years with diligency and alacrity comes within the power of but few.[22]

Giving his wife the ultimate credit, Robert Grattan Jr. believed, "The amount of heroism ought not to be estimated by the magnitude, but by the number of sacrifices."[23] By his standard, Patsy Minor Grattan was a true hero.

Although the death of George Gilmer of Lethe paid many of the Grattans' debts, he was mourned by many. Robert Jr. described the man's character at length: "I am of the opinion that Uncle Gilmer was the best educated man I ever saw.... There was no man whose family and friends had a more unshaken confidence in, and no one to whom they were drawn with a more kindly affection. Every one loved him because he loved everyone."[24]

The gentle nature of the owner of "Lethe" seems to have been reflected in his dealings with his slaves and even his horse. According to another nephew, one of the servants, "Great Billie," was held in high esteem. When the slave died, the older Gilmer sold several animals and gave the funds to Billie's children. As for the horse "Sorrel," he was treated as a pet, first at Lethe and then by the Grattans at Contentment. Then Gilmer continues,

For the last twenty years of his life, he rode a noble horse of his own raising. Sorrel never was in harness. He carried master wherever he went, especially once a week during the summer months across the Shenandoah River, to the top of the Blue Ridge Mountain, where he salted his cattle. Sorrel was never known to leave him, though often without confinement. When his master died, Sorrel was carried from Lethe to [Contentment], where he continued to be served by Major Grattan's children as if he were akin to them. Only the youngest was ever put upon his back. When he was, Sorrel would walk about with as much care as if he knew the preciousness of what he carried. Occasionally he would leave his pasture and go to Lethe, as if in search of something he had lost. He was always sent for as soon as missed lest he should suffer for the want of food. Sorrel lived to be twenty-seven years old. When he died, Major Grattan's children and grandchildren buried him with the greatest affection, as if he had been the last remnant of their good uncle.[25]

The generosity of both the owner of "Lethe" and Mrs. Lucy Gilmer Minor ended the indebtedness of the Grattans.

The Grattan family was in transition in the 1830s, with the younger adults marrying and leaving home and the birth of a new generation. Lucy, Robert Jr.'s very helpful sister, delayed marriage until she was twenty-seven. Peachy Ridgway Grattan, who had married before the family's financial crisis, moved in 1835 to Richmond, opening a very successful legal practice. John Grattan, the youngest sibling, went to study at the University of Virginia in 1832. He then studied medicine in Philadelphia. Moving later to Alabama, he established a successful medical practice before his early death. For the next several decades, family leadership revolved around Peachy and his wife, Jane Ferguson Grattan, Robert Jr. and Patsy Minor Grattan, and their older sister Eliza along with her husband George R. Gilmer. The last generation of Grattans to live at Contentment on the Shenandoah River, was born to Robert Jr. and Patsy. They had nine children, including Charles, born in 1833, Lucy Gilmer Grattan in 1835, George Gilmer Grattan in 1839, Robert Ridgway Grattan in 1841, and Peter Minor Grattan in 1843. All of these sons would live to serve in the Civil War; Lucy would marry a well-known Confederate officer. The fate of the younger children was troubled. One died as an infant and one died as a young adult. Only the last child, yet another John Grattan, would live into middle age. Born on June 21, 1853, he was too young to serve in the army, and thus was the only male in the fourth generation of Grattans who did not fight for the Confederacy.

The births of so many children added to the burdens of caring for elderly relatives. Keenly aware of what this meant for Patsy, Robert, Jr. rejected overtures to run for state office. "I had too many to whom I owned [sic] obligations of the strongest kind to permit me to think of such a thing… For many years I had my mother and father and Old Aunt Lucy Gilmer, to take care of, and to have left my wife with … a large and growing family would have been an injustice."[26] Very mindful of these limitations, Robert Grattan Jr. focused upon his family and local interests.

A lengthy account of Robert Jr.'s life from the 1850s omits three important topics. Although Robert Grattan described having attended a major conference to develop turnpikes, he never elaborated upon the building of the Valley pike between Staunton and Harrisonburg. Its construction led to the replacement of the stage road and the building of a bridge across the North River. To avoid floods, the turnpike company moved the road from the lowlands that were close to Contentment up the hill several blocks to the west. For the first time in its history the house was no longer buffeted by road noise, or, in dry weather, clouds of dust. Women and all the servants must have rejoiced. The new route left one curiosity, however. The stage road circled the hill and the Grattan family cemetery faced it. Perhaps in death old John Grattan may have wanted to keep an eye on the flow of travelers as he had in life. Now with the road removed and straightened in the late 1830s, the old cemetery was left an island in a field, surrounded by crops in the spring and summer much as it is today.

Robert Grattan's autobiography mentions his brother-in-law and friend George R. Gilmer. Gilmer served three terms in Congress and two terms as governor of Georgia, but Grattan never explained Gilmer's rise to the top of state politics. This rise to prominence is a somewhat complicated story—a story that, by the way, included the meaningful participation of Gilmer's wife, Eliza Grattan. Robert's older sister joined her husband when he campaigned for public office. She continued to be his confidant in political affairs and in writing the book that would bring them fame.

Eliza's unusual role in her husband's life grew out of her extraordinary upbringing. As a child, she was sent to Richmond to receive a formal education that included serious academic subjects. Even more importantly, Eliza Grattan lived with her cousin, Elizabeth Gamble Wirt, and with, of course, William Wirt. By dwelling in the Wirt household, she observed the nature of their marriage, one based upon the meaningful partnership of both spouses in decision-making, suggesting romantic love between equals. In Richmond, Eliza also saw the equally extraordinary relationship between Elizabeth Wirt's parents, Catherine and Robert Gamble. After Robert's death, the young woman watched Catherine's continued business success. When Eliza Grattan married George R. Gilmer, the couple pursed a companionate marriage as a romantic ideal. But unlike many young men and women of the time, they had role models close at hand.

Eliza Gilmer determined the social calendar of her husband. The former governor's explanation of how this came to be is very revealing:

> [On a journey to visit my relations in Alabama] my wife insisted that I should direct the time and place of our visitings, as I had always urged upon her to do when we were among her relations in Virginia. The day we left home, she began to prescribe where we should dine, and where we should sup, &c. I laughingly reminded her of her previous proposal, that I should

control our visiting until our return home. She replied, that she did not intend but that my absolutism should commence till we got to Alabama; if I so desired, she was content. She declined accepting any invitations, referring every one to me. When the applications were accordingly made, I did not know what she wanted, and, as that was which I wished to do, I was very much bothered. The third night after we retired to bed, I told her I was tired to death doing as I pleased, and that if she ever told me again to do so, I would not forgive her. She has constantly kept in mind this injunction.[27]

Eliza was also a quiet participant in the political strife that unfolded over the next two decades. In the years after their marriage, ill will developed between George R. Gilmer, then seated in Congress, and the Governor of Georgia, John Forsyth. Their disdain for each other became public. After Gilmer was reelected in the fall of 1828, Forsyth issued a proclamation "announcing the names of those elected to Congress" and requiring them to send him a letter of acceptance. When Gilmer failed to send the governor a letter, Forsyth issued a second proclamation "calling for a new election to be held" since Gilmer had violated state election laws. This skullduggery led to a series of interchanges between the governor and the congressman. When Gilmer admitted that he had made a mistake, Forsyth swept that apology aside. As the charges and counter charges increased, it became clear to many Georgians that Forsyth had selectively used parts of election law against Gilmer while ignoring other sections. The governor never relented in his course of action, but Gilmer eventually transformed the entire argument. Gilmer, probably with Eliza's blessing, issued one last letter on the topic. He resigned his seat in Congress, stating that Forsyth was forcing him to be a "selfish professional politician." Rather than joining this corrupt group, Gilmer chose to end his political career. He wrote, "I prefer becoming a private citizen."[28]

Since Gilmer was highly regarded, this created quite a sensation. The outcry even came from Columbia, South Carolina, where one newspaper observed, "Mr. Gilmer ... is one of the boldest and most candid men in Congress, and deserves well of the South for his consistent and manly defense of its rights and interests." A newspaper in Salisbury responded, "Mr. Gilmer was, in our estimation, the ablest man from Georgia, in the last Congress."[29]

As public pressure grew in 1829, Forsyth engaged in yet another political trick. He delayed announcing his bid for reelection. With both the governorship and a U.S. senate seat open, he waited until the last minute, declared for the senate race, and encouraged a friend to run for governor. This news traveled to a gathering of party leaders attending a University of Georgia commencement. Realizing what was happening, they pressured Gilmer into running for governor. In the election that followed, even the opposition party endorsed George R. Gilmer. Consequently, Gilmer soundly defeated Forsyth's candidate by two votes to one.[30]

Once he was elected governor, Gilmer and his wife quickly found themselves in a situation far more difficult than that of handling Forsyth's games. The complicated status of Native Americans in Georgia would cause ripples all the way to U.S. Supreme Court—a case in which the Cherokees obtained the legal services of William Wirt. This meant that Robert Grattan Jr. was in the horrifying position of seeing the husband of his first cousin, Wirt, sue the state governed by his sister's husband. In writing his own autobiography, Grattan avoided mention of the entire nightmare. While he might have felt comfortable in doing this twenty years later, in the early 1830s, the Shenandoah Valley would have been abuzz. Wirt's relationship with the Gilmers, the Gambles, and the Grattans was known. There were those who also knew that Eliza Grattan Gilmer, the First Lady of Georgia, had lived in the Wirts' household when she studied in Richmond. Worse, the dispute drew national attention.

The trouble began in 1829 after gold was discovered on Cherokee land northwest of Atlanta, drawing thousands of prospectors to the region. After a detachment of army troops proved ineffective in removing the trespassers, Gilmer issued a proclamation ordering both the gold miners and the Indians to stop digging. The governor later admitted, "I found paper bullets but light artillery against masses of men who could not read."[31] In the difficulties that ensued, the state sought to have whites on Native American soil swear allegiance to Georgia or leave. Some missionaries noted that the Cherokees and their land were under Federal jurisdiction, not state, and objected to Georgia's new law. This set the stage for the arrest of missionaries, including Samuel Worcester. Having been ill-treated by state lawmen, the missionaries and the Cherokees turned to Federal courts for protection, suing the State of Georgia. Once they obtained the services of William Wirt, Worcester and the Cherokees were on the way to the U. S. Supreme Court.

William Wirt corresponded directly with George R. Gilmer on June 4, 1830. The attorney began his letter by extending an olive branch:

A just respect for the State of Georgia, and a desire to avoid a misconstruction, which might be attended with evil consequences, seems to me to call for a communication, which, under other circumstances, might well be deemed officious and intrusive. The excitement with regard to the Indians within your borders is already so high, and in this state of feeling measures of the most innocent character are so easily misapprehended and converted into causes of offence, that I ...[hope] your Excellency will ...[see] this letter as a measure of peace.[32]

Wirt then proceeded to trace the history of his involvement for George and Eliza Gilmer. The Cherokee nation had serious questions about its treaties with the U.S. government and whether or not it was subject to the laws and regulations of the State of Georgia. Wirt expressed his support for the Native Americans, explaining:

It is my misfortune to differ with the constituted authorities of the State of Georgia on the question of her power to extend her laws into the Cherokee nation; and the late debates in Congress will have satisfied your Excellency that in this opinion I am not singular, but that I hold it in common with many of the most distinguished lawyers on our continent. [Wirt added], We may be wrong; and, as infallibility is not the lot of mortals, those who hold the opposite opinion may be wrong. Fortunately, there exists a tribunal before which this difference of opinion may be quietly and peaceably settled, and to this tribunal I think it may be regularly referred.... In the Supreme Court of the United States we shall find a tribunal as impartial and as enlightened as can be expected on this earth.[33]

William Wirt proceeded to factually describe the Cherokees to Gilmers as civilized and educated. He wrote,

They wear our dress, speak our language correctly, and in their manners indicate all the mildness and much of the culture and courtesy of our own best circles. They assure me that their people at home have abandoned the habits of savage life, and subsist by agriculture and the other usual and peaceful pursuits of civilized societies. They profess, and I believe with entire sincerity, to be willing to make the question of their rights under treaties, questions of pure law for the decision of our courts. [Wirt ended his letter by seeking Georgia's active participation.] The decision may be expedited by making a case by consent, if that course should suit the views of the State of Georgia.[34]

Having honestly assessed the lives of many Cherokees, Wirt sent copies of his letter to Gilmer, President Andrew Jackson, and the Cherokee delegation.

Although Wirt's suggestion may appear reasonable, he was not offering a level playing field. With a national reputation and years of litigation in front of the Supreme Court, Wirt knew it would have been difficult for Georgia to obtain counsel with the same experience and renown. Moreover, John Marshall still served as chief justice. Under his leadership the Supreme Court had sided with the Federal government, giving deference to its powers. The combination suggests that Wirt was trying to lure the Georgia governor into a courtroom battle he would lose or to scare Georgia away from defending itself. To Wirt's credit, the Cherokees and Samuel Worcester had a strong case and he was willing to pursue it with vigor.

Wirt's letter to the governor failed to recognize any familial relationship he had with the Gilmers. To a couple steeped in family heritage, the letter was offensive. The governor later wrote,

I had never felt so indignant as I did upon reading Mr. Wirt's letter...Mr. Wirt's first wife was my kinswoman...[I remember when] Mr. Wirt was poor, unknown, and undistinguished, when Dr. Gilmer took him into his house, gave him his daughter, and introduced him into the society of his friends.... Soon after the death of his first wife, Mr. Wirt removed to Richmond and then to Norfolk, and was in danger of being utterly ruined by dissipation, when he again prospered by marrying the daughter of Colonel Gamble of Richmond, my wife's first cousin. My wife lived with Mr. Wirt's family in Richmond when she was a little girl going to school.[35]

To the Gilmers' dismay, the local newspaper published Wirt's letter. The public responded with protest marches, warning the Gilmers not to accept Wirt's offer. Or as the Governor put it, "The people assembled en mass, paraded before my house with drum and fife, and noisy acclamations."[36]

To escape from this legal and political cauldron, George R. Gilmer embraced states' rights. He wrote a local justice, "We desire no decision of that [Supreme] Court to sustain the sovereign rights of the State. They rest upon higher authority—the power which necessarily belonged to the State when it became independent, and which it retained, when the Constitution of the United States was formed."[37] With this in mind, he thought that Georgia should not participant in the Worcester case. If the court rendered an unfavorable decision, his government would not recognize it. As Gilmer put it, "There is...no probability that the State of Georgia would submit to the orders of the Court if it should determine that the laws of the State in relation to the Indians were void."[38]

Samuel Worcester, the Cherokees, and William Wirt, of course, pursued the suit. In the January term of 1832, the Supreme Court heard the case and the Chief Justice John Marshall delivered the opinion of the court: "The Indian nations had always been considered as distinct, independent political communities, retaining their original natural rights, as the undisputed possessors of the soil, from time immemorial." Earlier in the nineteenth century, Georgia, itself had recognized this fact. In 1802, it acquiesced to the "universal conviction that the Indian nations possessed a full right to the lands they occupied" and "they possessed rights with which no state could interfere." Marshall concluded,

> The Cherokee nation, then, is a distinct community occupying its own territory, with boundaries accurately described, in which the laws of Georgia can have no force, and which the citizens of Georgia have no right to enter.... The whole intercourse between the United States and this nation, is, by our constitution and laws, vested in the government of the United States. [As a consequence,] the act of the state of Georgia, under which the plaintiff was prosecuted, is consequently void.[39]

The fallout from the Worcester case was complicated. Gilmer and his successors ignored the court's ruling. In time, the state repealed its law, released the missionaries, and compensated them for the loss of their property. The claim of state rights went unchallenged since the Supreme Court's decision was never enforced. President Jackson, of course, wanted Native Americans removed from the South and was not about to help them. This information was evidently shared with George Gilmer who observed that Jackson had been "prompt" in acknowledging "the rights of this State to extend its laws over all its territory."[40] It should be noted that although President Jackson would concur with Gilmer on this issue, he would reject state rights as it was pursued in South Carolina over the issue of tariffs. Whereas Jackson would be long remembered for defending the Federal government against states' rights, few realize that he had tarnished his own reputation in Georgia.

The Cherokees were eventually forced to leave Georgia, leading to an enormous loss of life. Of the 16, 000 who left the state, only 11,721 reached their new home in Oklahoma—their number reduced due to disease, malnutrition, and the hardship of the journey. When the "Trail of Tears," as the Cherokees called it, occurred in 1838 neither John Marshall nor William Wirt were still living. The aged chief justice had died on July 6, 1835, and the distinguished attorney on February 18, 1834.[41]

William Wirt's death was unexpected, and he left his wife with financial burdens that exceeded Robert Grattan's at Contentment. One of the few assets was a largely undeveloped cotton plantation in Florida. Elizabeth Gamble Wirt joined her brothers in the Tallahassee area and gradually converted a mountain of debts into an estate worth $70,000. Elizabeth Wirt obviously possessed the remarkable financial skills of her mother.[42]

For George and Eliza Gilmer, the Worcester case left no permanent political damage. Although Gilmer lost his bid for reelection in 1831, he retained considerable rapport with the electorate, for he was returned to the U.S. House of Representatives and then again to the governorship in 1837. For him to have survived the ups and downs of the period suggests that he possessed considerable political skill. As one biographer wrote, George Gilmer had a "solid character, common sense" and "industrious habits."[43] His opposition to the Cherokees, however, suggests that he caved in to political expediency. In this, other state leaders joined him, including the governors of the period. Unfortunately for Native Americans, the wishes of the local aristocracy prevailed.

The turmoil of the 1830s took a toll on the governor, undermining his health. Rather than submitting to the often brutal treatment of doctors of the period, Gilmer turned to his wife for medical care. As one might expect, Eliza Grattan Gilmer treated him with great care, lancing boils and removing rotting teeth. As he recalled, "When a tooth became so decayed as to break, my wife cut out the pieces. She would take each fragment, and cut round it so softly with her little fingers, that what would have been insufferable from the hard hands of a doctor, scarcely occasioned any pain when done by her. The suffering was usually forgotten in the pleasure which I felt from observing the great effort she made to avoid hurting me."[44]

Acting as her husband's primary caregiver, Eliza Grattan Gilmer interceded with a well-known physician in Philadelphia. The doctor offered advice that included "go to the mountains," which the couple interpreted as "go home to the Shenandoah Valley."[45] The couple went and stayed at Contentment and recuperated among their kin. By this time, George Gilmer and Robert Grattan Jr. had already found a topic of mutual interest—agricultural improvement. Later, as the president of a regional agricultural association, the former governor would observe, "We must not only discover some way of renewing the primitive richness of our exhausted lands, but force them to produce more than they did in their virgin freshness." He added that to do this required bringing together "a great mass of agricultural knowledge, science, and experience."[46]

Robert Grattan Jr. fully agreed with these sentiments; he experimented not only with soil restoration but also with livestock. The swine at Contentment in 1828 were so inbred as to be worthless. As Robert Jr. recalled, "When I purchased my farm, I purchased the hogs on it. They had been on the farm for twenty years, and had bred in and in, until they had become dwarfed and diseased. The first lot of pigs…I could not fatten." To remedy this situation, he turned to other farmers. "I purchased of Corbin Warwick, two pigs from his Goochland estate, of the Surry stock. I was on a visit to my Sister and Dr. Harris, and he took me down to Mr. Warwick's farm to see some fine Durham cattle…. But I was very much pleased with his Surry hogs, and of the opinion that they were the best hogs I have ever handled."[47] Not content with just these animals, Robert Grattan Jr. upgraded all of the livestock at Contentment. It is not surprising that a writer in the nineteenth century referred to him as "one of the most successful and intelligent farmers of the State."[48]

By the end of the 1830s, Robert Grattan Jr. found time for politics—he and his sister and his brother-in-law turned their backs on the Democratic Party. In his autobiography, he wrote:

In the summer of 1840, George Gilmer and Franklin Minor [another brother-in-law] and their wives met here, and we had many discussions as to the proper choice of President, between Gen. Harrison and Mr. Van Buren. We all had the same opinions, upon the policy of the government, and the only question was as to who [m] would be most likely, to carry out our particular views.... The administration of Mr. Van Buren, had been so corrupt.... This was the view that George Gilmer and Mr. Minor took. I never had a doubt that Gen. Harrison would be compelled to accept the policy of the great mass of those who would elect him. We had discussed the subject until I had become excited on the subject, and in the fall I was induced to go into a political meeting, where I was called upon for a speech. Never having made a political speech, I had no expectation of anything of the sort, but the call was such that I was compelled to say something...I have never made as popular a speech since. The next spring, I was urged warmly to become a candidate for the legislature.[49]

George R. Gilmer offered his own explanation for rejecting Van Buren. "I considered it better for the country to have honest men to administer the Government without clearly defined political principles, than those who professed well, but acted badly." In the ensuing election, the former governor stood as an elector for the Whig candidates, Harrison and Tyler. The Democratic Party could not fail to notice Gilmer's association with its opponents. As he put it, "I was elected, made President of the Electoral College, and proclaimed the result of the election, that all of the votes of Georgia were given for William Henry Harrison to be President and John Tyler to be Vice President."[50] This act finished Gilmer's political career—not that it seems to have bothered him.

Eliza Grattan Gilmer shared her husband's willingness to act. In Lexington, Georgia, the school of higher education was Meson Academy. It had been funded in 1806 from the will of Francis Meson. Meson left both money—some $8,000—and considerable valuable land as an endowment. From these resources had been erected an impressive building. It was described by a historian, "as handsome and commodious as any academic building in the state—among educational structures excelled only by Franklin College, completed in 1805, which was the sole building on the University of Georgia campus." After almost forty years of use, the trustees of Meson academy voted to demolish the building. The same source continues: Hearing this news, Mrs. Gilmer "ordered her carriage and immediately hurried to the place where the Trustees were meeting and 'told them that would never do: that the Academy endowed by Meson must never be torn down or removed.' Mrs. Gilmer's appeal was sufficient to cause the Board to rescind its action, and for the next fifty years and more the academy building continued to serve the purpose for which it had been constructed."[51]

Eliza Gilmer's brother's achievements were also significant. By the middle of the 1850s, Robert Grattan Jr.'s position in the Shenandoah Valley rivaled his grandfather's. Debts had been retired and lush fields had replaced the eroded acres found there in the 1820s. In pursuing economic solvency, Robert Grattan Jr. returned to the frugality of his forebears while adopting agricultural innovations. He was obviously very proud of his achievements and those of his closest relatives. The results of his efforts were impressive. One historian described Grattan's possessions: "The 1850 Federal census valued his land [1,000 acres, six hundred of which were improved] at $45,000. In addition to his land, he owned 18 slaves, 18 horses, 10 cows, 81 head of cattle, 1,400 bushels of wheat, 1,500 bushels of corn and a water powered mill in which 10,000 bushels of grain were stored."[52]

Notes:

1. Grattan, "Manuscript of Major Robert Grattan, Jr," 23-24.
2. Gilmer, *Sketches*, 33.
3. *Rockingham County Deed Book* 7, 352.
4. Grattan, "Manuscript of Major Robert Grattan Jr.," 23.
5. Ibid., 20-21.
6. Ibid., 21.
7. Ibid.
8. Peachy R. Grattan Diary, August 19, September 19, 1826.
9. Burnt Deed Book 7, Rockingham County, Virginia, 352.
10. Grattan, "Manuscript of Major Robert Grattan, Jr.," 22.
11. Peachy R. Grattan Diary, April 20, 1828.
12. Grattan, "Manuscript of Major Robert Grattan, Jr.," 24.
13. Ibid., 28.
14. Ibid., 29.
15. Ibid., 25.
16. Ibid., 26.
17. Ibid., 11.
18. Ibid., 23.
19. Ibid.,25.
20. Ibid., 30.
21. Ibid. 29.
22. Ibid..
23. Ibid..
24. Ibid., 11.
25. Gilmer, *Sketches*, 18.
26. Grattan, "Manuscript," 34.
27. Gilmer, *Sketches*, 365.
28. Coulter, "The Dispute over George R. Gilmer's Elections, 175.
29. Ibid., 183.
30. Skelton, "The States Rights Movement in Georgia, 1825-1850," 104.
31. Gilmer, *Sketches*, 278.
32. Ibid., 271
33. Ibid., 272.
34. Ibid.
35. Ibid., 275.
36. Ibid., 276.
37. Ibid., 277.
38. Ibid.
39. Samuel A. Worcester, "Plaintiff in Error v. the State of Georgia."

40. Gilmer, *Sketches*, 360.

41. Collins, "Activities of the Missionaries Among the Cherokee," 322.

42. Jabour, *Marriage in the Early Republic*, 167.

43. Cook, *Governors of Georgia, 1754-1995*, 107.

44. Gilmer, *Sketches*, 384-385.

45. Ibid., 386.

46. Ibid., 456.

47. Grattan, "Manuscript," 33.

48. "Rockingham County Personals," *Hardesty's Encyclopedia*, 1884, 24.

49. Grattan, "Manuscript," 33-34.

50. Gilmer, *Sketches*, 44.

51. Coulter, "Meson Academy, Lexington, Georgia," 126.

52. May, *Life Under Four Flags*, 305. Between the sale of slaves in 1827 and the census of 1850, the population of African-Americans at "Contentment" returned to the pre-sale number. This probably reflects a natural increase in the population.

6. College and Secession: 1851–1861

The issues that gave birth to the Civil War divided not only the nation, but also families in the Shenandoah Valley. The Grattans were not exceptions. In the 1840s and 50s, Robert Grattan Jr. never acted upon his political interests beyond serving as a justice of the peace. Yet at the same time, his lively discourses with George and Eliza Gilmer created an environment of political awareness for his children. Among the children who were listening were Charles Grattan, the eldest son, and his brother George Gilmer Grattan, five years younger. Charles was almost seven when his father and uncles left the Democratic Party to support William Henry Harrison. These times were exciting, making a lasting impression on the child. For his younger brother, politics probably could not have been avoided. George was named for the Georgia governor—a man who had no children. Subsequent events suggest that the Georgia couple came to view this child as their heir.

From Robert Grattan Jr.'s autobiography and the published statements of George R. Gilmer, it is possible to outline family views on the issues of their era. As Democrats, both men rejected high tariffs advocated by early industrialists. Tariffs placed duties on imported goods, including cloth. During Andrew Jackson's presidency, the national bank became the focus of strife. While both Robert Grattan Jr. and Gilmer rejected the bank, they wanted it closed in an orderly fashion. As Gilmer recalled, "I was opposed to rechartering the bank, and yet did not approve of the means used by General Jackson [President Andrew Jackson] for putting it down." When the president withdrew funds, he went too far too fast. The governor expressed his disapproval: "The measure was high-handed, and the means used not according to rule."[1] Beyond these long-standing issues, both families took a keen interest in public education. Robert Grattan Jr. never forgot the haphazard teachers of his youth or his own struggles in providing for his children. Gilmer, on the other hand, spent many years as a trustee of the University of

Georgia. He expressed regret that other issues kept him from spending more time on education during his terms as governor. "The …support of free schools, and the education of the poor, was a matter of great difficulty when I was in the Executive Department." Writing the legislature, he encouraged the "appropriation of large sums of public money" for the "education of the people."[2]

On the topic of slavery, both men held a position that differed from many Southerners. Robert Grattan Jr., as he put it, wanted "to have nothing to do with Negroes" but was compelled by family debts to manage them. Robert was alienated from his slaves, a situation he aggravated by selling part of them in late 1820s. Afterwards, the number of slaves at Contentment returned to 18 in 1850. Robert's misgivings were also echoed in Georgia. One modern historian believes that George R. Gilmer moved to Lexington to practice law to avoid deriving his livelihood from agriculture. He "shunned wealth based on plantation slavery."[3] But this is only part of the story. Imagine an antebellum governor of Georgia claiming as Gilmer did, " I had never bought negroes, or made profit out of their labor, accumulated any money by speculation, cultivated cotton, or been engaged in any way in the occupations which were stimulating them to incessant exertions."[4]

While both Robert Grattan Jr. and George R. Gilmer disliked slavery, they rejected racial equality and abolition. By themselves, the governor believed, African-Americans were "incapable of self-government and self-improvement." Yet under white leadership, blacks prospered. He continued, "When infants, they are our fond nurses; in childhood, our playmates; and in after life, our obedient and willing servants."[5] By never acting upon his antipathy for slavery, Robert Jr. remained one of the largest slave owners in Rockingham County, while the former governor minimized entanglement in his private life, he supported the status quo in public.

Beyond these positions, Robert Grattan Jr. and George R. Gilmer identified with states' rights. The governor had seen his own position rejected by the U.S. Supreme Court and sustained by President Jackson. It is thus easy to understand why the States' Rights Party chose Gilmer as a potential elector in the Electoral College. For Georgians who assumed that Gilmer would join them in their support of secession, though, a shock awaited. The former governor compared the situation to divisions in the Bible: "The dealings of God with the Israelites of old were given to us for our instruction. Let us profit by them. The twelve tribes separated from each other. The ten were lost, utterly extinguished from the face of the earth, so that not even a remnant can be found. The other two have been scattered over the whole world, to be a byword and a reproach. We, too, have been the favored people of God; have been preserved, and have prospered beyond any other people." Then Gilmer reminded Georgians of the oaths they had taken. "We have all at some time...taken an oath to support the Constitution which has for sixty years held the States together. We will observe the solemn requirements of that oath." Then the old Scotch-Irishman drove his message home. "The ark of our Covenant is in danger. Let us remember our obligations to protect it."[6]

George Gilmer's message was not well received by some Georgians. As he put it, "I soon found myself out of place."[7] Like the Scots of old, including Catherine Grattan Gamble, he pressed on. A biographer observed that Gilmer's creed included not caring about "the consequences."[8] This attitude spilled over to his and his wife's last project. They decided to write a history of the settlement of the Lexington and Athens area of Georgia. To make this possible, Eliza pressured her brother and cousins to write family histories. Although most of this material was never used, the couple did write *Sketches of Some of the First Settlers of Upper Georgia*. The product was, as a historian put it, an "interesting and gossipy book."[9] It was also brutally honest—a trait that did not spare family members. Gilmer described his own father as obese and lazy: "He was very fat from childhood, weighing at the age of eighteen two hundred pounds. He floated on water without any effort, except straightening his legs. The school to which he went when a boy was up the Shenandoah River, a mile or two from his father's. During the summer months he went home by floating and swimming down the river, to save himself from walking." As he aged, Thomas M. Gilmer only gained weight. "He continued to grow more and more corpulent."[10]

From family, the Gilmers turned to discussing their former neighbors in both Georgia and Virginia. Micajah McGehee, for instance, knew nothing of books.[11] The writers also noted, "When he was young, it took drinking all day to make him drunk. When he was old, he got drunk twice a day. After he became a member of the Methodist Church during the great religious excitement of 1809–11, he still continued to get drunk. When he was spoken to about it, he said that the habit was so confirmed that he could not live without the free use of brandy. He was requested to say what quantity was necessary for his health. He agreed to try to limit himself to a quart a day, but the allowance failed to keep him alive."[12] The Gilmers found Richard Taliaferro to be "deformed—

his legs and thighs being only a span or two long, whilst his body was of ordinary length and size, and his head unusually large. His mind was of good capacity, but his deformity so soured his temper, and mortified his pride, as to drive him from society."[13] Meriwether Lewis, the Gilmers reported, secretly discovered a gold mine on his famous expedition to the Pacific. "Fact," however, was "not made public." This might explain his untimely death. The Gilmers wrote, "In the morning his throat was found cut, and he dead; whether by his own hand, or others in search of his account of the place where the gold was to be found."[14] In the public outburst that followed the publication of the Gilmers' book, no one doubted their veracity. It was just far, far too candid for comfort. Families scurried to find copies to burn—all to the amusement of George and Eliza Gilmer.

Robert Grattan Jr.

There have been many reactions to the Gilmers' book from historians. E. Merton Coulter, Professor of History and then Regents Professor Emeritus of History at the University of Georgia, refers to it as "famous."[15] John Wayland at James Madison University describes it as "a great book."[16] The Gilmers were remarkably deft at portraying human frailty with a large dose of humor. *The Dictionary of American Biography* in the 1930's said it possessed an "ingenuous frankness."[17] It is not surprising, then, that Gilmer's *Sketches* was reprinted in 1926, 1965, 1992, 1995, and 1999. And after over 150 years, it is still in print.

Alas, this season of mirth that George and Eliza enjoyed in 1855 was short-lived, interrupted by the shocking death of Robert Grattan Jr., from typhoid fever. As an adult, his health had been robust, unlike the former governor. The physical problems of his childhood had disappeared. In spite of this pattern, on August 6th of that year he died. All of the Grattan possessions were left to his widow, Martha "Patsy" Minor Grattan. If there was any comfort for her, it came from its being the summer season, which meant that her eldest child, Charles, was home from the University of Virginia. In 1855, sons Charles,

Martha "Patsy" Minor Grattan

George G., Robert R., Peter M., and John were respectively 22, 16, 14, 12, and 2 years of age. The daughters, Lucy G., Mary E., and Louisa N., were 20, 8, and 5.

The unexpected death of Robert Grattan Jr. interrupted his son's university studies. A year would pass before Charles resumed classes at the University of Virginia. His educational choice grew out of a combination of talent and family preferences. Charles's father, Robert Grattan Jr., valued a course of study written by the university's first professor of law, Francis Walker Gilmer. Gilmer made a long-lasting and very favorable impression on Robert Jr. Important connections to the University of Virginia also came through Charles's mother. Patsy Minor was a cousin of

George R. Gilmer

John Barbee Minor, the fourth person appointed Professor of Law there. Minor was to have an exceptional career, beginning well before the Civil War and stretching across half of the nineteenth century. As one biographer put it, he was "preeminent in legal education, he established the high position of the law school of the University of Virginia among American law schools."[18] Originally an opponent of secession, John Barbee Minor helped to get Federal protection for the school at the end of the Civil War. Consequently, the University, unlike Virginia Military Institute, was never looted or burned. With such distinguished relatives, it is easy to understand that Charles Grattan and his brothers were expected to attend the University in Charlottesville—a tradition that would continue for generations to come.

Even with the incomplete records that exist, it is possible to trace Charles Grattan's studies at the University of Virginia. In 1853 and 1854, he took classes in mathematics, natural science, and chemistry. In 1856, Charles undertook courses in political economy and law, earning "proficiency" in each of these areas. Charles's younger brother, George Gilmer Grattan, followed his brother's example in 1857–1858. But unlike the eldest son, he continued his education at the University of Georgia. By the end of the 1850s, George R. Gilmer's health deteriorated yet again.

Elizabeth "Eliza" Grattan Gilmer

George Gilmer Grattan

Seeking emotional support, Eliza turned to her family on North River, requesting that her husband's namesake. George Gilmer Grattan, the Grattans' second son, leave for Lexington. The prospect of starting a law career under the guidance of a former governor promised an opportunity that could not be missed. Sadly for both Eliza and her nephew, the former governor died on November 15, 1859. This did not keep the younger man from being admitted to the bar the next year in Georgia on October 16, 1860.[19]

By the beginning of the Civil War, many of John Grattan's grandchildren were dead. This included half of Catherine Grattan Gamble's children: Elizabeth Gamble Wirt and John Grattan Gamble.[20] Their sister, Agnes "Nancy" Cabell, lived until February, 15, 1863. The same pattern continued in the Shenandoah Valley where Robert Grattan Jr., had died. His brother, Peachy, however, would work as an attorney in Richmond for more than a decade to come. Their older sister, Eliza Grattan Gilmer, would see the end of the Civil War.

His father's death thrust Charles Grattan into family leadership. When this happened, he was comparatively younger than his father with a better formal education, and far fewer liabilities. He also seems to have had his grandfather's fondness for social groups. This claim is supported by a newspaper description of Charles from 1902: He "was a well educated man and well read in general literature. He was a good speaker and a good writer. He was quick, sprightly and more or less versatile. He was a man of wit and humor; and as a raconteur was delightful."[21] Long on stories, Charles could entertain and amuse others at great length.

Charles's love of social interaction brought him into contact with a wide assortment of students at the University of Virginia, many of whom were secessionists. In 1861, a newspaper described Charles Grattan as a pragmatic secessionist—something that put him at odds with older family members. College life then as now introduces the young to new ideas, and it was a lively place for the ferment of political opinion. It is less clear that George joined in his brother's newfound perspective— for he was more reflective than Charles. George "possessed an innate gentleness of spirit, which coupled with a marked courtesy of manner, made him stand out among men. In his personality was embodied a rare combination of sweetness and strength that commanded love and respect from all."[22] Even if George became a secessionist, in Georgia there were plenty of people who would have reminded him of his aunt and uncle's position. Near the end of their book, the Gilmers exclaimed: "Now is the time for patriots to come...to the help of their country."[23]

When Charles Grattan returned home from college, he was eager to begin a career in politics. In 1859, he ran for General Assembly of Virginia and won. For the first time since the eighteenth century, a family member was elected to the state legislature. Charles no doubt savored both his victory and his arrival in Richmond. He must also have been aware of the similarity of the timing of his and his ancestor's election, for his great-grandfather had represented Rockingham County at an uncertain time during the American Revolution. In 1779, the British had begun a major campaign for victory. As Charles assumed his duties in Richmond, the United States was, in 1859, in the midst of sectional turmoil. The government of President James Buchanan proved its ineptness daily.

The Grattans watched national issues emerge from the admission of new states to the building of railroads, triggering sectional responses. Differences of opinion even swirled within families and communities. In the Shenandoah Valley, close to the borders between regions, people held very different views from each other, to which they attached a host of emotions. The local newspaper, the *Rockingham Register,* offers a perspective on the period and the complexities in which Charles Grattan maneuvered. The paper started 1861 by rejecting the beginning of the Declaration of Independence. The phrase "all men are created equal" was, as the *Register* put it, "a doctrine false in its statement and pernicious in its tendency."[24] South Carolina had already seceded, but had yet to be joined by other states. The *Register* blamed South Carolina's actions on Yankees:

> And what fearful cause has produced such disastrous effects....the fanaticism of the North. She has heaped every species of insult upon her sister States of the South. For a long time her legislatures have totally ignored the Constitution, and enacted laws repugnant to its provisions and oppressive to the South. Her Greeleys ... of the press, her Beechers ... in the pulpit, her Sewards and Sumners in her legislative halls, turning aside from their legitimate pursuits, have united

in waging an unholy and heaven-cursed crusade against Southern institutions. With hearts overflowing with pseudo-philanthropy, they have neglected the wants and interests of their white slaves, and sought with pious zeal to better the condition of a race infinitely more happy and contented than thousands in their own midst. Unmindful of the beam in the northern eye, they have presumptuously sought to pluck the mote out of the Southern eye. And thus the South has been goaded to that point where forbearance ceases to be a virtue.[25]

Charles Grattan probably agreed with the newspaper's conclusions: "This state of things cannot long continue. Upon this point, the South is united. We are not prepared to submit longer to the officious intermeddling...of the North. The issue has been made and must now be met. The question must now be settled and settled forever." Yet the paper stopped short of advocating secession outright. "We demand only our constitutional rights, and these we will have in the Union, if possible, out of it, if necessary. We are not in favor of disunion for the sake of disunion." [26]

Several days later, Charles Grattan voted for the following resolution along with 111 members of the house of representatives. Five members voted No: "Resolved by the General Assembly of Virginia, that the Union being formed by the assent of the sovereign states respectively, and being consistent only with freedom and republican institutions guaranteed to each, cannot and ought not to be maintained by force. The government of the Union has no power to declare or make war against any of the states which have been its constituent members."[27]

Several weeks later, Charles Grattan supported another house resolution: "Resolved by the General Assembly of Virginia, that if all efforts to reconcile the unhappy differences existing between the two sections of the country, should prove to be abortive, then, in the opinion of the General Assembly, every consideration of honor and interest demand that Virginia shall unite her destiny with the slave holding states of the South."[28] Charles Grattan was joined by 106 others while few voted against the motion.

By this time in January 1861, four states had joined South Carolina in seceding—Mississippi on the 9th, Florida on the 10th, Alabama on the 11th, and Georgia on the 19th. Two others, Louisiana and Texas, followed on the 26th and on February 1st. After this frenzy of activity came a pause, for neither Virginia nor North Carolina acted. In the Shenandoah Valley, the *Rockingham Register* reported a meeting of Unionists. On the 29th of January, a group met at Mill Creek and approved the following resolutions:

1. Resolved, That we declare ourselves second to none in devotion to the Union of the States, being out and out Union men.
2. Resolved, That the Federal and State officers are in the main filled with men who take extreme positions on abstract questions, and whom seem willing to plunge the country into war to carry them out.
3. Resolved, That we are opposed to the eternal cry of disunion. It is fraught with evil. Disunion cures nothing, and for which we would be reproached by posterity.
4. Resolved, That we deeply deplore the present agitation on the subject of slavery, especially in Congress, and will gladly give our sanction to any just and constitutional measures which will forever take the subject out of the hands of that body.
5. Resolved, That we take our stand against breaking up, and the re-constructing of the Constitution and the Union. We are for compromise. Both sections have been guilty of wrong.
6. Resolved, That unfortunately the country is cursed with a portion of the rabid, the restless, the excitable, and the rampant. If nothing will do them but fight, let them fight alone. We advise the people to keep cool, stay at home, attend their business, and be peaceable. The excitement should be calmed, not increased.
7. That we declare our opposition to all schemes of secession, as a means of preserving the Union. We caution the people against such deception. It is [co] operating with firebrands, and may prove [deadly]."[29]

While the Grattans heard such sentiments in the Valley, a convention to consider secession was called and potential delegates ran for seats. In early February, a leading Unionist in Rockingham County withdrew on the eve of the election. At that time, the *Register* believed that George H. Chrisman was "the very embodiment " of union sentiments. Before withdrawing, Chrisman had canvassed the area, noting local preferences. "I was confirmed in my first impressions. In relation to the eastern side of the county, I was satisfied that I would receive but little support from that side." Even in Port Republic where Chrisman was known, enthusiasm for the Union had disappeared: "The votes of a few personal friends were all that could be counted on with confidence." The situation in the western half of Rockingham County was very different though: "My own neighborhood, however, was with me unanimously, and I went around with the candidates to Ottobine and Bridgewater. In this district, my prospects were bright." In the end, Chrisman dropped his candidacy, fearing that the pro-Union vote would be divided between too many candidates. He concluded his efforts by attacking Charles Grattan and complimenting his Mennonite and German Baptist neighbors, "I am thankful to you all, and doubly thankful to my German friends, who came…to my support, with a degree of confidence and unanimity that is without example."[30]

Even though George H. Chrisman took the position that the "dissolution of the Union" would be the "destruction of all remedies," he did not convince his own son of this.[31] A newspaper from 1915 reports that his son George D. Chrisman, by this time in 1861, had already raised a volunteer company of infantry.[32] If this is true, then it is an example of secession tearing families apart in Rockingham County—a tragic characteristic of the war to come. The younger Chrisman would, of course, be remembered for his service as a Confederate officer. Making his sentiments final after the war, he would marry Charles Grattan's sister, Lucy.

As a leading local secessionist, Charles Grattan responded to the elder Chrisman, and the *Rockingham Register* printed his letter on March 1, 1861. By this date, the Confederacy had already formed a government and inaugurated Jefferson Davis as its president. The swiftness of these actions cut the ground from under those willing to compromise. As a pragmatic secessionist, Charles Grattan described the situation for the citizens of Rockingham County. States had already seceded and armies were being raised by the Federal government. "Coercion," as he put it, will "be attempted" and consequently "the border states" will be the "field of battle." But who would be in this army? "The myrmidons of John Brown" will "march through your soil, among your negroes and barns, to feed on your supplies." Worse, they would expect you to join this army and your taxes will go to pay for it. The war will be paid for from increases in tariffs which "you must pay."[33]

Charles expressed willingness to compromise with the North. "The best [answer], according to my way of thinking, is a sectional Senate. Whenever any measure which will infringe unjustly, either upon the north or south, is proposed…they may call a vote by sections, and if two-thirds of the members from either section vote against the measure, it fails to pass. This would defeat unjust tariffs, unconstitutional Pacific railroads [and] unconstitutional land grants." Such a system "would carry us back to the golden days of the Republic, because it would stop the crusade against slavery, as it presents an insuperable barrier to its overthrow."[34] Yet this was not the peace proposal that was the most discussed of the time—the ideas of Senator Crittenden. By rejecting Crittenden, Charles Grattan maneuvered voters toward secession.

He ended his letter to the *Register*: "It is with great sorrow that I learn through you [George H. Chrisman], that a large portion of my people are dissatisfied with my course. I cannot believe it is through misapprehension. I regard the safety of the people, in person and property, as the supreme law, above party of all kind. In a Union properly administered, I believe we could enjoy it, and therefore I expressed my willingness, in a card, to vote for either of the three opponents of Mr. Lincoln. I am of the same way of thinking still."[35] Yet this was long after the 1860 election, and Lincoln's inauguration was only a few weeks away.

The state convention in Virginia eventually passed a decision to leave the union and worked toward a pro forma referendum by the electorate. The absence of many pro-Union votes in Rockingham County suggests a combination of coercion, which one historian noted at Mt. Crawford, and discouragement. At the same time, a historian notes that the "firing at Fort Sumter had clearly swung many Virginians ... to the side of secession."[36] The presence of just a few No votes let the *Register* trumpet on May 24th, "There are no traitors to Virginia in this part of the Old Dominion."[37] Virginia joined the Civil War with a newly reelected Charles Grattan in its legislature. The Grattan family had helped lead Rockingham County into the conflict.

In the tumult, the Grattans let February 17, 1861, pass without notice. Older family members, if they had still been living, would have recognized the date—for it was the centennial anniversary of the purchase of their farm on the North River. On that date in 1761, George III had been on the British throne for a year. A century later the United States was on the eve of the Lincoln Presidency. Shortly before the Armageddon, George R. Gilmer recorded his sentiments about the family's ancestral home:

> During our stay at Contentment
> Very soon one morning I went,
> To the highest top the hill,

Which overlooks the house and mill.
Gazed at the River passing by,
And the mountains on all sides high,
Traced the well shaded pleasant walk,
Where Betsey and I used to talk
And the flat rock where we set,
Then warm lips and warmer hearts met
And realized how strong may be
The sweet pleasures of memory.
Then standing I became lost in thought
And all surrounding things as naught.
Objects then seen in fancies dream
Like real things were made to seem.
I saw the tall form, and bright face,
Of the sire of our Grattan race;
And his firm wife, holding his hand,
To his long life's last ebbing sand;
And then turning where they lie,
Memory brought many a sigh.[38]

Notes:

1. Gilmer, *Sketches*, 379, 378.
2. Ibid., 345, 348.
3. Cook, *The Governors of Georgia, 1754-1995*, 105.
4. Gilmer, *Sketches*, 366.
5. Bryson, *The Virginia Law Reporters Before 1880*, 67.
6. Gilmer, *Sketches*, 451.
7. Ibid.
8. Cook, *The Governors of Georgia*, 107.
9. Ibid.
10. Gilmer, *Sketches*, 13.
11. Ibid. 128.
12. Ibid., 128-129.
13. Ibid.. 126.
14. Ibid., 83-84.
15. Coulter, "David Meriwether of Virginia and Georgia," 32
16. Wayland, Historic *Houses of Northern Virginia*, 227.
17. *Dictionary of American Biography*, Volume 7, 307.
18. *Dictionary of American Biography*, Volume 11, 26.
19. The license is owned by the family of George Gilmer Grattan, IV.
20. Each of the following grandchildren died in the 1850s: John Grattan Gamble in 1853 and Elizabeth Gamble Wirt on January 27, 1857.
21. *Rockingham Register*, June 27, 1902.
22. *Daily News-Record* (Harrisonburg, Va.), November 1, 1915.
23. Gilmer, *Sketches*, 451.
24. *Rockingham Register*, January 4, 1861.
25. Ibid.
26. Ibid.
27. *Journal of the House of Delegates of the State of Virginia, Extra Session, 1861*, 9.
28. Ibid., 10.
29. *Rockingham Register*, February 8, 1861.
30. Ibid.
31. Ibid.
32. *Daily News-Record*, Nov. 24, 1915,
33. *Rockingham Register*, March 1, 1861.
34. Ibid.
35. Ibid.
36. Long, *The Civil War Day by Day: An Almanac*, 60.
37. *Rockingham Register*, May 24, 1861.
38. Excerpt from George R. Gilmer's "Album," Grattan Family Papers, Collection of Martha Townes Grattan and George Gilmer Grattan IV.

7. The Grattans in the Civil War, 1861–1864

All of the adult sons of Patsy and Robert Grattan Jr. served in the Civil War and saw action in a range of battles, from such famous ones as Chancellorsville and the Wilderness to smaller ones like Olustee in Florida. Two of the four men, Charles and George, wrote descriptions of the war that date from just after Appomattox to the twentieth century. The most widely known account was written by Charles about Stonewall Jackson at Harpers Ferry at the beginning of Civil War.

In the spring of 1861, Charles Grattan probably joined Virginia officials in assuming that Harpers Ferry was key to keeping the Shenandoah Valley out of Union hands. From looking at two-dimensional maps, it would have seemed strategically significant since it stood at the juncture of the Shenandoah and Potomac rivers, overlooking rail lines to Washington, D.C. With the potential of Federal military action looming, the state sent a combination of militia and volunteer units to the village. From the middle of April until after the arrival of Thomas "Stonewall" Jackson two weeks later, Harpers Ferry became more of a circus than a staging ground. As the various units arrived, they found a place that could not be militarily defended. Harpers Ferry lies in a ravine with bluffs on three sides: a military force with heavy artillery could shell such a poorly situated place into oblivion. This unnerving fact seems to have made little impression on raw recruits or much of the militia. When Charles Grattan arrived in late April with a Staunton militia unit, he had already begun a friendship with John A. Harman. Grattan recalled: "On our way down [the Valley], Major Harman informed me that he was to occupy the position of Quarter Master…and asked me to assist him. I being willing to do anything to aid the cause, readily consented, thinking in my extremely fresh condition, that the only duty of a Q. M. [Quarter Master] was to find a place to camp and sleep the troops. I did not apprehend much trouble, or that my attention would be seriously directed from the prominent object, that of killing Yankees. I was mistaken in this as in many other notions I entertained about war and things pertaining thereto."[1]

Harman rapidly put Charles Grattan to work in myriad of tasks.[2] As Charles recalled:

We did not have a single copy of Army regulations in our office and if an officer had come to me with a regulation I should have thought he was putting on airs and wanted taking down.

One thing the Major had though, that was indomitable energy, and push, with a very good share of good sense, and this energy he infused into all the boys in his office. He bought everything he could lay his hands on and turned it over to the needy commands daily arriving, depending upon his office force to keep him straight, we trying by a sort of military double entry to do so. The Major did not confine himself to Q. M. [Quarter Master] supplies, but bought and issued commissaries as well, made and fitted up caissons and did anything that no one else did and that meant pretty much all. In fact we did not know where the line was that divided the different fields and had no guide but our own crude ideas of the varied wants of the troops daily coming in with nothing.

It goes without saying that we were worked day and night, but that did not matter so long as we were permitted to hope, we would soon be allowed to try our hand on the Yankees as we called them and every one of the assistant Quarter Masters clerks like old settlers in the Indian days, worked day and night with his musket within reach and on one or two occasions we were summoned to arms by false summons of the approach of an enemy. I think it was the universal dread that the war would close before we had a chance to drive the Yankees from the sacred soil.[3]

From the busy, productive quartermaster's office Charles Grattan occasionally watched the ostentatious generals from the militia units. In his well-known biography of Jackson, historian James I. Robertson cited Charles's observations:

Each one of four generals had the regulation staff and as

many additional aids, adjutants and inspector generals as he had friends and that each one of these was ornamented according to his taste and ability to acquire, with spurs, cocked hats, feathers, epaulets, sashes, &c. and armed with pistols, swords, sabers, and what not, it is easily conceived what an incongruous mass it was if there was a divinity that shaped their ends the rough hewing had been badly done.[4]

According to Robertson, a command structure did not really exist beyond one-hundred-man companies. The remainder of the garrison seems to have been as poorly prepared. As the historian put it, "Guard details were a farce, despite daily false alarms. There was little equipment, less ammunition, and deep shortages of supplies... Hundreds of volunteers wanting to be soldiers packed the village and waited for some sense of direction while B&O trains rumbled through town regularly loaded with coal and other raw materials for Union mobilization."[5]

Charles was not alone in recognizing the ineptness of militia officers. No doubt having reached the same conclusion, the governor of Virginia ordered officers above the rank of captain to surrender their posts to regular army officers. When Col. Thomas J. Jackson arrived in Harpers Ferry at the end of April, he had authority to remove all of the peacocks and begin organizing Valley troops into a fighting force. While the task was daunting, Jackson himself brought to it the stolid persona exemplified by his plain clothing for which he would become known. According to Robertson, he wore the "blue uniform of a VMI faculty member, with neither insignia nor gold lace on the faded coat...with the faded cadet cap tilted over his eyes and seemingly blocking all vision save what was at his feet."[6]

Jackson brought with him a small staff and once he arrived in the village, he began adding to it. He turned to VMI students he knew and to men who followed instructions with care and energy. The militia units had some talent and thus the quartermaster from Staunton caught his eye. As one explains, "Among the first additions was Major John A. Harman, a month younger than Jackson. Men came to call Harman 'the old Major,' and most people gave him a wide berth. Big-bodied, big-voiced, short-tempered and incredibly profane, Harman was not afraid of anything. He became Jackson's first and only quartermaster. Harman worked tirelessly at his job; he would have ordered Jackson himself out of the way if necessary to obey Jackson's orders."[7]

As a part of Harman's staff, Charles Grattan saw Jackson shaping raw recruits into soldiers. Very long working days replaced idleness and the regular afternoon parade. According to Robertson, "Seven hours of drill were part of the daily schedule. The area had few level places for marching, but Jackson took advantage of every clearing and sent the troops daily through every routine, including occasional cross-country tramps. The state of the weather was irrelevant. Early May was unusually wet and cool. One detachment marched twenty-four miles through a steady downpour and returned to camp 'thoroughly drenched and disgruntled.'"[8] As one might expect, the camp rapidly began turning into a real military post with real military training.

For a number of weeks, Charles Grattan dined with Thomas Jackson. This was not, to say the least, a pleasant social event. The soldier wrote,

The Col. and his staff …messed together. We took our meals in one of the government buildings on the hill, vacated by the late commandant or one of his subordinates. We of the Q. M. department were kept employed from daylight until late at night… but we did not grumble, we imagined we were performing a patriotic duty and our names would linger on the tongues of after ages. The only moments of relaxation we enjoyed were those we spent at meal time, but here we were met by the grave, solemn countenance of our Commanding Colonel: all were afraid of him. We ate as silent as mutes, ever and anon casting a stealthy eye upon the Col. to see if he ate like other men, or bolted raw meat and gnawed bloody bones. What was to be done? The Surgeon, the Adjutant, the Aid and all the others sat like oysters; they ate but spoke not. Who was to bell the cat? I the youngest declared my intention of getting off a joke at this festal board. My messmates held up their hands in holy horror and advised me against any such rashness: told me my doom would be the guard house at the least, and declared they would under no circumstances be considered participants in such reckless folly.[9]

Yet Charles was young and game. He recalled,

One day at dinner during the awful silence, unbroken but by the subdued rattle of the knives and crockery, I got off as a feeler a very diluted and mild joke. Not one of all that crowd of guzzlers even looked up or noticed I had said a word, but cut a glance at Col. Jackson out of the corners of their eyes to see what he would do. I suppose it was some time since the Col. had had a joke poked at him, for he evidently did not seem to know exactly what to do, had a half startled appearance, then subsided into a smile, then all those long faced Jeremiahs laughed, the ice was broken, we were all saved from dyspepsia and learned to esteem the genial qualities of our great Commander as we admired his wonderful genius.[10]

The daily routine at Harpers Ferry ended when orders arrived on July 13, 1861: Jackson's desire to abandon the village had been granted. The commander became famous for his rapid movements, and his abrupt departure from the community would foreshadow future events. Jackson and his troops spent much of the 13th preparing to depart and to destroy facilities with military value. A noted historian describes what happened next: "A quiet night ended on June 14 at 5 A.M., when a huge explosion echoed through the valley of the Potomac. The splendid 900 foot metal B&O railroad bridge was blown into rubble."[11] Jackson's troops then burned the armory, the rail depot, machine shops, and the telegraph office.

The quartermaster and his assistant, Charles Grattan, faced the daunting task of moving not only Jackson's military supplies to Winchester, some thirty miles south, but also everything in Harpers Ferry that an army might need. Keeping up with the future general was the nineteenth-century version of keeping up with George Patton during World War II. The pattern of rapid action was repeated in July. Thomas Jackson received a message at 1 A.M. on July 18th to join general Beauregard at Bull Run. At 1 P.M., he rode out of Winchester at the head of his brigade. Twelve hours later his force was still marching eastward. It had forded the Shenandoah River and crossed the Blue Ridge. By the time they rested, the general exhaustion was profound. James Robertson describes Jackson as throwing himself "upon a bed of leaves in a fence corner."[12] At 8 A.M., he and his troops were at a railroad station, and by late afternoon, they were transported to what would be a battlefield. An incredible forced march plus the railroad moved 2,600 men over 55 miles in less than thirty hours. Federal troops, of course, were as unaware of Jackson's movements as Beauregard, who could only express "shock" at his arrival.[13] Subsequent events suggest that the Southern general should have greeted Jackson more cordially since he and his brigade would save his army.

After a day of rest, Jackson and his Valley troops positioned themselves behind the middle of Confederate lines. On the morning of July 21, 1861, Federal troops under General Irvin McDowell forded Bull Run and attacked the left wing of the Southern army. By 9:30 A.M., more than 12,000 Union soldiers were grinding fewer than 4,000 Confederates under generals Nathan G. Evans and Barnard E. Bee up. As an important reserve, Jackson's brigade was ordered to reinforce Evans and Bee. He rushed his men forward but did not thrust them into the crumbling lines. Instead, he hid them in woods behind the crest of Henry Hill. This gave his troops some protection while leaving an open field of fire. As Federal troops swept Evans's and Bee's troops back, they found themselves confronted with Jackson's stationary position. Despite numerous efforts, they could not dislodge his men. Observing the scene, Barnard Bee gave Jackson the name "Stonewall." By 4 P.M., Confederate forces launched new attacks, while McDowell ordered a Union retreat. His exhausted, green troops were unprepared for such a decision and the Federal army collapsed into a sea of fleeing soldiers. The Confederate victory left both armies disorganized and there was little subsequent military action. Afterwards, Jackson and his brigade camped near the battlefield for some months.

Given the rapidity of Jackson's trip to Manassas and the innumerable tasks for the quartermaster's staff, it seems probable that Charles Grattan did not reach Manassas until after the battle. In any case, he continued his duties with Harman into the fall of 1861, when he returned to his seat in the state legislature. Still hoping for combat duty, he used the opportunity to study for an artillery exam.

When Charles Grattan reached Richmond in December 1861, he found the city packed with soldiers and politicians. Unlike thousands desperately seeking accommodations, he simply went to his uncle's home—no doubt an interesting experience since Peachy Ridgway Grattan was a member of the Richmond City Council. Peachy, of course, had moved to the capital in 1835. Six years later he began supplementing his law practice as the court reporter for the Virginia Supreme Court. For the next thirty-nine years, until his death in 1881, he labored to record 33 volumes of legal opinions that were published as the *Grattan Reports*. In doing this, Peachy Grattan exercised great care, seldom injecting his own views. In the twentieth century, a historian commented on his service in a turbulent age. "It is interesting to note that he retained his position before, during, and after the Confederacy and Reconstruction. This alone must be regarded as a personal tribute to his integrity and to his competence."[14]

In 1857, at the age of 56, Peachy Grattan ran a successful campaign for public office. He followed this victory with additional ones in 1858, 1860, 1861, and 1862.[15] Thus, the eldest living male member of the Grattan family capped his political career in 1865 by winning seats on the Richmond City Council and in the House of Delegates. By doing so, he became the third member of his family to join the state legislature.

In late 1861, Peachy's double victory remained in the future, but even so, he and his nephew, Charles, had cause to savor the late 1850s and early 1860s. Both men knew that their family's position in the Shenandoah Valley and in Richmond rivaled Catherine Grattan Gamble's half a century earlier. In keeping with this trend, Charles Grattan was an active representative.

The most important piece of legislation associated with Charles Grattan appeared in March 1862. The Civil War was obviously going to be longer than anticipated, and many residents of Rockingham County were Mennonites and German Baptists. Recognizing the needs of these churches whose theology was based upon nonviolence, he made a motion in the house on the 24th of March requesting exemptions from military service for "those persons whose religious tenets forbid them bearing arms."[16] Evidently this released legislation that had already been drafted. During the required three readings, an effort to block the bill was successfully beaten back on March 27, 1862. The House then held a roll call vote. Those in favor of granting exemptions based upon religion won easily—79 ayes to 18 nays. Charles Grattan, of course, voted in the affirmative, and the House of Delegates "ordered" him to carry the legislation to the Senate "and request their concurrence."[17] The Senate, according to historian C. E. May, amended the House's bill, adding a requirement that a religious objector "pay a lump sum of $500 plus a two per cent tax of his property, or serve as a teamster or in some other noncombat capacity...."[18] The House agreed to the Senate's changes and the bill became law.

Charles was helped in his efforts to protect the rights of conscientious objectors. It had been preceded by lobbying from German Baptist elders and by petitions signed by their congregations and many Mennonites. As one would expect, the new law gave "much satisfaction." It was noted that many of the more affluent began paying the $500 fee. For those less fortunate, Stonewall Jackson honored the legislation. His biographer James Robertson describes the general's policy: "No man had deeper respect for religious beliefs than did Jackson." Consequently, he followed Virginia's legislation to the letter: "Male members of pacifistic sects would enter the army, be organized into units, and learn the rudiments of drill short of the point of firing weapons. They would then serve as teamsters and in other support roles for soldiers on the front lines."[19]

To the dismay of pacifists and of Charles Grattan, the Confederate government superseded the Virginia law by passing its own conscription regulations, ignoring the plight of German Baptists, Mennonites, and Quakers. For some Southerners who valued states' rights, it was also offensive. In addition, the people who had paid the fees lost their money. Or, as C. E. May put it, "they had been had."[20] The predicament, of course, did not go away. German Baptists and Mennonites fled to Pennsylvania or faced renewed persecution.

When his term ended in March 1863, Charles Grattan took his artillery exam and passed, receiving the third highest score. This led to a promotion from sergeant to first lieutenant and orders to join Col. Henry C. Cabell's battalion of artillery. While this was not a bad assignment, for Cabell was one of William H. Cabell's children and a cousin, Charles preferred to serve with Valley troops. He approached a Major Allan who seems to have gotten Stonewall Jackson's approval. In spite of these efforts, Charles was not reassigned until the fall. In the meantime, his service at Chancellorsville received commendation from several officers. Henry Cabell noted in his report, "I desire to call attention to the gallant conduct and energy and efficiency of Lieutenant Grattan, my ordnance officer."[21] These comments were echoed by Major S. P. Hamilton: "Lieutenant Grattan, ordnance officer, performed his very arduous duties with the greatest zeal and efficiency, and is worthy of special praise."[22] In October 1863, some months after Gettysburg, Charles received a promotion to captain and was reassigned to J.E.B. Stuart's staff. This assignment took him into a series of skirmishes in November. On the 29th, the famous general noted, Grattan's "horse was killed [beneath him] at Parker's Store."[23]

After Stuart's units went into winter quarters in December 1863, Charles Grattan applied for a furlough. The captain had been courting Elizabeth Crawford Finley, and they both wished to be married. Records describe General Stuart's response. The request was granted with the following endorsement written in Stuart's hand:

> Hd Qrs Cav. Corps
>
>   27 Dec. 1863
> Approved and respectfully forwarded as Capt. G's business is very urgent & cannot be transacted by proxy.
>
>   J. E. B. Stuart
>   Major Genl.'[24]

Charles appreciated Stuart's humor and candor, keeping the note as a treasured memento.

As indicated earlier, Charles was not the only son of Robert Grattan Jr. to write firsthand accounts of the Civil War. Additional descriptions come from the pen of George Gilmer Grattan. Charles's younger brother was not with Stonewall Jackson or J.E.B. Stuart, but he served as a staff officer for a much longer period. A resident of Georgia, George enlisted in Atlanta in May 1861 in what would become company K of the 6th Georgia Infantry. As a lieutenant, he served under Col. Alfred Colquitt. When Colquitt became a general in 1862, George became his aide-de-camp and then "assistant adjutant general." The 6th Georgia Infantry fought in a long series of famous engagements, from Maryland and Virginia to a battle in Florida. The reason for such diverse service will soon become apparent.

George Grattan's service with the 6th Georgia infantry proved to be very different from his brother's on Stonewall Jackson's quartermaster corps. Although Colquitt did not display Jackson's personal reticence, the fighting became especially grim. One of George Grattan's fellow officers, William Fisher Plane, led Company H as its captain. It is very likely that Plane's experiences paralleled George's. After an early engagement, Captain Plane recorded the ugliness of war. In a letter to his wife he wrote:

Thursday, June 5, 1862

I cannot describe the battlefield. The first I ever saw. I would to God it could be the last & our country saved. The dying and the dead, the rebel & the Federal side by side. The groans of the wounded & the lifeless corpse of the foe prostrate on the field, half covered with water. Here the body pierced through. Here the brains issuing from the head. Here the lifeless body. Who trods a battle ground, but shrinks at the thought, that he too may find a resting place there.[25]

A month later, William Plane wrote about the fighting near Richmond that George Grattan knew firsthand: "I pray God that the battles may be over & peace returned to our mourning country. Out of the 350 men we carried into action, 206 were killed and wounded. Our losses are heavy, but we have done much for our country & put to flight & whipped in nearly a dozen battles the boasted army of the North, 'so splendidly equipped.'"[26]

On July 8, 1862, Plane again offered a graphic account of combat to his family:

But dearest, its one thing to read of battles, another to be an actor in the Strife, & behold the scenes of anguish & of pain, the dead and the dying, & those not mortally wounded, to hear the cries of distress, and untold pain. None can realize the horrors of war, save those actually engaged. The dead lying all around, your foes unburied to the last, horses & wagons & troops passing heedlessly along, rushing to overtake the foe in his retreat, and to give him battle again. The stiffened bodies lie, grasping in death, the arms they bravely bore, with glazed eyes, and features blackened by rapid decay. Here sits one against a tree in motionless stare. Another has his head leaning against a stump, his hands over his head. They have paid the last penalty. They have fought their last battle. The air is putrid with decaying bodies of men & horses. My God, My God, what a scourge is war.[27]

George Grattan's own description of the war followed Plane's, dealing with events a few months later. When Robert E. Lee began his invasion of Maryland, before the Battle of Antietam, he divided his army into several parts. This information, without the knowledge of Confederate generals, fell into Federal hands and ended up in the possession of General George McClellan. Consequently, McClellan started moving his army with uncharacteristic speed. On the 13th of September, he wired President Lincoln, stating, "I have all the plans of the rebels, and will catch them in their own trap, if my men are equal to the emergency." He hoped to catch Lee's forces separated by the Potomac River, and as McClellan wrote one officer, "cut the enemy in two, and beat him in detail."[28]

By the 13th of September, Colquitt and Grattan had led their brigade across the Potomac and marched into a pass on South Mountain. South Mountain begins at the river, slightly east of Harpers Ferry and runs off to the northeast, forming a ridge between Frederick, Maryland, to the east and Antietam to the west. Roads from Frederick crossed South Mountain at Boonsboro Gap, which was closest to the town, and at Crampton's Gap, some fifteen miles or so to the south. In the afternoon, General D. H. Hill, Colquitt's superior, ordered his troops to guard Boonsboro Gap. As the 6th Georgia Infantry passed through the Gap, J.E.B. Stuart's cavalry, returning from the east, met it. When Colquitt asked Stuart about Federal troops, George Grattan heard the answer: "My distinct recollection is that General Stuart reported that there were no troops following him but Cavalry...."[29] Therefore, when the Georgian asked for reinforcements, his request was brushed aside. After the cavalry passed, the 6th Georgia Infantry marched halfway down the slope, forming a skirmish line across the road.

Spending the night on South Mountain revealed a very different reality from Stuart's report. As George recalled, the valley below became lighted with "with campfires....When these campfires continued to increase as the night advanced, Col. Colquitt became satisfied that there was a very large force in his front, and he sent a courier with a note to General Hill giving this information. Before daylight General Daniel Harvey Hill appeared on the mountain top, and being soon convinced that Colquitt's information was correct, sent orders to the other brigades of his division...and also informed General Lee of the situation."[30]

Within less than an hour, Colquitt and Grattan placed four regiments next to the 6th Georgia Infantry in a line across the road. At one end, next to a cliff, came the 28th and then the 23rd Georgia Infantry, followed by Colquitt's home unit in the middle, and then came the 27th Georgia and the 13th Alabama. Since the small army could be flanked on the Alabama end, Colquitt withdrew a company of sharpshooters from each of the Georgia regiments, and spread them out further up the ridge beyond the vulnerable wing.

About breakfast-time, additional Southern troops arrived, a brigade led by General Garland. This force Hill sent off to guard a minor gap a mile or so to the south. By the time General Garland reached Fox's Gap, Federal troops had bypassed the main Confederate formation and met him as he arrived. As George Grattan recalled, "General Garland had little time to put his regiments in position before he was attacked by the brigade of Scammon and Crook.... In this first attack General Garland was killed, and his brigade was somewhat broken and divided."[31] One regiment, the 5th North Carolina continued fighting from the north side of the pass while three others rallied on the south side. The number of Federal troops greatly exceeded the Confederate and the remnants of Garland's brigade began falling back. Trying to slow the Federal advance, General Hill rushed forward several artillery pieces and the last of his soldiers—he was down to the "staff officers, teamsters, cooks, and stragglers...."[32]

The way was now clear for a Federal victory—for if they should pour troops through Fox's Gap, then Colquitt and Grattan's troops at nearby Boonesboro Gap would have fled or faced being surrounded. Quick action could have driven Union troops across South Mountain by 9:30 or 10:00 am. Yet it did not happen. McClellan's army was missing a chance to destroy Lee's divided army. As George Grattan put it, "fortunately for us their evident timidity caused them to delay...."[33] This permitted the arrival of another southern brigade— which General D. H. Hill sent into the cauldron. Only very desperate fighting held Federal troops in check at Fox's Gap.

The rest of Hill's force at Boonesboro Gap, though, faced its worst pressure later in the day. George Grattan writes, "About three o'clock in the afternoon General McClellan ordered an advance of all his troops...."[34] At first Federal troops tried to flank the Alabama end of Colquitt's line. The sharpshooters, using the cover of boulders, greeted them, as Grattan put it, with "a most disastrous fire." Or as Colquitt recalled, "As the enemy advanced, these skirmishers poured upon his flank a sudden and unexpected fire."[35] After retreating, Union troops attacked the opposite end of the southern formation. They sent an entire brigade against two Georgia regiments. Again and again they "rushed upon the 23rd and 28th...in the fiercest assaults...."[36]

Only the arrival of reinforcements at 3:30 P.M. began to brighten the desperate situation. Even so, the final Federal attacks on the 28th Georgia Infantry led to the use of the last of their ammunition. As a consequence, its colonel ordered the fixing of bayonets. The battle of South Mountain reached its last critical moment. McClellan's troops could now break thorough Confederate lines. Then Grattan describes an amazing event: "Immediately there was a lull in the Federal firing in his front, and soon the enemy ceased firing altogether...."[37]

Before the arrival of the reinforcements, Daniel Harvey Hill's small army had held off an immense Federal force. George Grattan recorded this astounding achievement, "Not over 4,000 men beating back...more than ten times the number of the enemy."[38] In modern times, the historian James I. Robertson used the term "Thermopylean-type contest" to describe the struggle on South Mountain.[39] It was an amazing accomplishment, yet few would remember it. The struggle resumed in the evening with Colquitt and Hill eventually withdrawing west toward Antietam. Their actions on South Mountain would rapidly be overshadowed by the famous battle—not changing the fact that the smaller struggle had strategic implications. Stonewall Jackson would have time to finish his capture of over 12,000 Federal troops in Harpers Ferry, and Lee would be able to regroup his army. As yet another historian observed, D. H. Hill "accomplished all that was required."[40]

George Grattan and Alfred Colquitt survived Antietam—or Sharpsburg, as Southerners called it. At Antietam, more than 23,000 Americans were killed or wounded in a single day of slaughter, the worst in this nation's history. Afterwards, Colquitt wrote the following letter to the wife of William Fisher Plane:

My dear Madam, In the battle of Sharpsburg your husband fell by a shot from the enemy while endeavoring to carry Col. Newton from the field who had been seriously wounded. It is the decided testimony of the men of his company that the shot was fatal. The enemy late in the day held the ground upon which we fought and hence his body as well as many others were within the lines of the enemy. On the day following there was a brief cessation of hostilities to bury the dead & remove the wounded, but no one was allowed to pass inside the picket line of the enemy. We could not certainly ascertain his fate, but particular inquiries were of the Federal officers & those who were detailed to bury the dead, and I am satisfied with the accurate description given that he was buried by them. I would be most happy if it were in my power to hold out to you the hope that he was wounded and is now in the hands of the enemy. It is possible that may be the case, but it is my conviction from all the facts that he was killed.

I sincerely sympathize with you in your bereavement, and I regret that I cannot do more to alleviate your distress than offer you the assurance of my sympathy. The grace of God alone can alleviate our afflictions or make us resigned under such losses. Very respectfully yours truly, A. H. Colquitt.[41]

Thus a man who forthrightly and accurately recorded the brutality of war perished in it on September 17, 1862.

Similar condolences were sent to families of officers in Colquitt's brigade, for George Grattan lost many of his friends. A modern historian writes, "Colquitt had gone in with 10 field officers; 4 were killed, 5 badly wounded, and the tenth had been stunned by a shell."[42] The general's own report echoes these results: "In this sharp and unequal conflict I lost many of my best officers and one-half the men in the ranks." The dead included Colonel L. B. Smith, of the 27th Georgia, Colonel W. P.

Barclay, of the 23rd, and Lieutenant-Colonel J. M. Newton, commanding the 6th Georgia—all of whom fell at the head of their regiments. "Their loss is irreparable. Upon every battlefield they had distinguished themselves for coolness and gallantry." Colquitt ended his report with praise for his young assistant, "Lieutenant Grattan, my aide-de-camp, was conspicuously bold in the midst of danger and untiring in the discharge of his duties. I cannot here mention the names of all, dead and living, who are entitled to a tribute at my hands."[43]

In the spring of 1863, Colquitt's reputation changed dramatically at Chancellorsville. While leading one of Stonewall Jackson's columns, the Georgian spotted Federal troops. Historian James Robertson describes a sequence of events: "On a May evening in the Virginia Wilderness, indecision overcame Colquitt. He disobeyed Jackson's strongest order and halted his brigade to meet the 'threat' on his front and flank. Colquitt's standstill removed Jackson's right from the attack. The Georgian not only neutralized his own brigade; when Colquitt stopped his troops blocked Ramseur's brigade behind him and isolated the Stonewall Brigade."[44]

When this happened, Robertson notes, "Ramseur raced to the trouble spot. Finding no Union troops, he made his way angrily to Colquitt. Continue the advance, he shouted; he would guard the flank. Yet it was too late to correct the line. Colquitt's unauthorized halt removed a fourth of Jackson's men from action. Now only 15,000 men in six brigades composed Jackson's attack."[45]

James Robertson is not alone in describing these events. Those who study the Civil War and military strategy explain: "Colquitt's advance along the right was the least obstructed either by woods or enemy troops. But his error took his and Ramseur's men out of the attack… that meant only six of the 15 brigades in Jackson's force carried the initial assault. Colquitt slowed the advance on the right…. That removed any chance of enveloping the Union positions from both sides, and possibly capturing whole units with their artillery."[46]

After the battle, Colquitt's brigade was withdrawn from the Virginia front and sent to the Carolinas and then to Georgia, where it saw little action until 1864. Furgurson notes the real consequence of this change. "Had Colquitt…not been transferred…he would have had to face a court of inquiry."[47]

While George Grattan was serving with Colquitt, his younger brothers also saw action. In 1861, Robert, twenty years of age, and Peter, eighteen, enlisted in the First Virginia Cavalry. As a prophetic witness to coming events, a letter from Robert survives from March 28, 1862: "Dear Mother, I received your and Peter's letter only a day or so ago…We are living on unsifted meal and fat meat fried on sticks. [He soon adds.] We are living without any tents."[48] The combination of such diets and exposure no doubt contributed to the subsequent poor health of both men. Sadly, Robert lost a battle with typhoid fever and died at home on Dec. 28, 1862. Brother Peter would be hospitalized in Charlottesville for part of May and all of June 1862. He was sick yet again in September and October—events that taxed the Grattan family, especially their mother Patsy.

Stress for Patsy Grattan and her daughters would have arisen from more than just these illnesses. Military action swept through the Shenandoah Valley. Federal troops under General Nathaniel Banks reached nearby Harrisonburg in early 1862 and then withdrew. In the spring of that year, Stonewall Jackson's Valley campaign took his army south along the Valley pike towards Staunton. Then, after a victory at McDowell, he returned, heading back towards Winchester. With two armies closing in on him, Jackson returned to the Harrisonburg area, fighting at Port Republic and Cross Keys. Both battlefields are close enough to Contentment for Patsy Grattan and her daughters to have heard cannon fire. Military threats for the remainder of 1862 and all of 1863 were far more rumors than substance. The local newspaper published many inaccurate reports about the Valley and distant battles. The most bizarre appeared on July 10, 1863:

There exists no longer a doubt about our having achieved a great, glorious, and overwhelming victory over the enemy at Gettysburg, Pa. The latest reports we have put the number of prisoners at 40,000. This is very probably an exaggeration. But that we have taken a very large number of prisoners is absolutely certain. The larger number of prisoners were taken on Sunday, by strategy, our forces under A. P. Hill pretending to retreat, when they were followed in hot haste by the Abolitionists. Suddenly Generals Ewell and Longstreet made flanking movements, closing in behind them, whilst Hill occupied their attention in front. The result was, that the whole of the pursuing force was 'bagged.' This will be found to be the correct version of the winding up of the struggle near Gettysburg.[49]

Evidence from the real battle reached Patsy Grattan's home, to the horror of its residents. As Lee retreated from Pennsylvania, wagons loaded with the wounded were ordered "up" the Valley turnpike. The roads were, of course, superior to other directions, creating less stress for the casualties. Yet the scale of the suffering is difficult to describe— the train of wagons stretched for seventeen miles—outstripping local capacities to respond. The Harrisonburg newspaper described the situation after Antietam:

> The public highway in the Valley of Virginia from Winchester to Staunton is now crowded with suffering, wounded soldiers…. These poor soldiers are wounded in almost every part of their bodies, some in feet, some in legs, and others in their hands, arms, and heads. They left the battlefield to make their way to some hospital or to their homes. Many of them are not able to hire a conveyance, whilst they are scarcely able to trudge along the wearisome and toilsome road which stretches out before them. Many of them, we doubt not, frequently suffer from hunger, thus almost every farmhouse by the wayside has been 'eaten out' by the numbers who throng this great highway of travel. It is an exceedingly painful sight to us to see these poor, ragged, toil-worn, battle-scarred heroes trudging wearily and painfully along, with the pangs of hunger added to their other afflictions. It is the duty of every man and woman in our once smiling and peaceful Valley to look to the comfort and welfare of these patriots. Many of them are native-born Virginians, whilst others come from other and distant States of the Confederacy. They are all our brothers and friends. Let the Valley maintain its ancient and well-known character for hospitality. It is an imperative duty prompted alike by the noblest patriotism and the most exalted sense of Christian obligation.[50]

By the end of 1863, most of the fighting in the Shenandoah Valley had occurred north of the Grattans' estate, Contentment. In 1864, violence shifted southward, engulfing the Grattans and their world.

Notes:

1. Charles Grattan, "Some Reminiscences of Camp Life with Stonewall Jackson—Before He was Known to Fame."
2. Robertson, *Stonewall Jackson*, 224.
3. Charles Grattan, "Some Reminiscences of Camp Life with Stonewall Jackson—Before He was Known to Fame." Manuscript in the Grattan Family Papers.
4. Robertson, *Stonewall Jackson*, 223.
5. Ibid.
6. Ibid., 224.
7. Ibid.
8. Ibid., 227.
9. Charles Grattan, "Some Reminiscences of Camp Life with Stonewall Jackson."
10. Ibid.,
11. Robertson, *Stonewall Jackson*, 243.
12. Ibid., 256.
13. Ibid., 257.
14. Bryson, *The Virginia Law Reporters before 1880*, 65.
15. Manarin, *Richmond at War: The Minutes of the City Council*, 186-1865, 629.
16. *Journal of the House of Delegates, 1862*, 308.
17. Ibid., 320.
18. May, *Life Under Four Flags*, 403.
19. Robertson, *Stonewall Jackson*, 337.
20. May, *Life Under Four Flags*, 404.
21. *War of the Rebellion*, Series 1, Vol. 37, 843.
22. Ibid., 845.
23. Ibid., Series 1, Vol. 29, 901.
24. Trout, *They Followed the Plume*, 155.
25. Lewis, "The Letters of William Fisher Plane," 227.
26. Ibid., 223.
27. Ibid..
28. Quoted in George G. Grattan's "Battle of Boonesboro Gap or South Mountain," 4.
29. Ibid., 5.
30. Ibid., 6.
31. Ibid.
32. Ibid., 8.
33. Ibid.
34. Ibid., 9.
35. *War of the Rebellion*, Series 1, Vol. 19, 1053.
36. Grattan, "Battle of Boonesboro Gap," 10.
37. Ibid.

38. Ibid.

39. Robertson, *Stonewall Jackson*, 601.

40. Roody, *The Georgia Volunteer Infantry*, 67.

41. Lewis, "The Letters of William Fisher Plane," 226-27.

42. Robertson, *Stonewall Jackson*, 723.

43. *War of the Rebellion*, Series 1, Vol. 19, 1054.

44. Robertson, *Stonewall Jackson*, 723.

45. Ibid.

46. Furgurson, *Chancellorsville*, 190.

47. Ibid.

48. Robert R. Grattan to Martha Minor Grattan, Grattan Family Papers.

49. *Rockingham Register*, July 10, 1863.

50. Ibid., Sept. 26, 1862.

8. A World Engulfed by War, 1864

The last full year of the war brought great extremes for the Grattans and left them divided. The Grattans and the Gilmers differed on the issue of secession, with part of the younger generation supporting it. The older family members remained Unionists, with George R. Gilmer publicly comparing leaving the Union with the Israelites who betrayed their faith. In the rush to Civil War, Charles Grattan had the luxury of not having to deal with either Gilmer or his father since both men were dead. The Grattan women were not so fortunate, since the remaining owner of Contentment had been the hostess for the many extended visits of the former Georgia governor. His wife was, of course, Patsy's sister-in-law, and George Gilmer was a cousin through her mother. With the notoriety that followed the publication of the Gilmers' book, Patsy Grattan's close relationship with both Gilmer and Eliza had grown ever brighter. Her daughter, Lucy, like the proceeding generations of Grattan women, had a mind of her own. With a great interest in current events, she took positions that she supported at length. Lucy sided with her old brother on succession, fully expecting the Confederacy to win.[1]

The older woman was not comforted when in the fall of 1863 a number of Confederate officers selected the area around Contentment for their winter headquarters. General Thomas L. Rosser picked nearby Grassy Dale, less than a mile to the south, while General John D. Imboden chose a place on the road between Mt. Crawford and Bridgewater.[2] After the Gettysburg campaign, Lee gave Imboden the valley district when there was little military activity. To him fell the task of patrolling and minimizing the effects of raiders and deserters. Hundreds of Confederate troops were camped within three miles of the Grattan home place; the Civil War was now at hand. The New Year began, leaving the mother and her eldest divided—one with the marked sense of foreboding and the other still believing victory was possible. For months the news alternated back and forth, giving rise to Patsy's worst fears and Lucy's expectations.

The first military action for the family in 1864 occurred in Florida and it was an excellent turn of events for the Confederacy. George Gilmer Grattan had been sent to Georgia with Alfred H. Colquitt. After a blunder at Chancellorsville, a cloud lingered over the brigade and its commander. In January or early February, it became apparent that a major Federal offensive would occur in Florida. A number of Floridians in several East Coast ports professed sympathy for the Union. These people eventually caught the attention of President Lincoln, claiming that it was possible to knock a Confederate state out of the war. A quick and easy Federal victory in Florida could have strengthened Lincoln's bid for reelection. To forestall such a possibility, Colquitt's brigade was quickly dispatched by rail, hoping to reinforce the meager local forces at hand.

In Florida, Colquitt and Grattan joined local forces led by Brigadier General Joseph Finegan.[3] This combined army easily defeated Federal troops at Olustee near Lake City. The consequences of Olustee were significant for the southern generals and their troops. The military reputations of both Finegan and Colquitt soared. Since their victory saved Florida's capital and its plantations from Federal troops, both men and their units were called to the front in Virginia.

There was a horrific ugliness to Olustee that few historians have noted. Scores of wounded African Americans were killed after the battle ended. George Grattan's published account offers clues to responsibility: "Immediately upon the commencement of the rout Gen. Colquitt had ordered the cavalry to the front in pursuit...By this time Gen. Finegan had arrived...and assumed command. He now directed Gen. Colquitt to leave one regiment in front as an advanced guard, and to lead the rest of his troops back to camp at Olustee station.[4] When this happened, Colquitt and most of his soldiers left the battlefield and marched away to the west. The disgrace of killing the wounded belonged to Finegan. Shortly after the battle Finegan admitted to Federal officers that he had "150 wounded prisoners, of whom three were Negroes." Then the general covered up the situation by saying, "ambulances were still engaged in removing the wounded from the field."[5]

The knowledge of Patsy Grattan at Contentment was limited to the news of a Confederate victory and George's return to Virginia. She had no reason to inquire about the treatment of wounded prisoners, and the soldier did not share what he knew. Yet such savagery may explain his subsequent behavior. Letters after the war indicate that George Grattan skipped veterans' reunions—a policy not explained by a lack of money, which was not the case.[6]

While George was returning to Virginia, his brother Charles went into the field as a part of J.E.B. Stuart's staff. In the spring of 1864, the well-known Theodore S. Garnet recorded a brief encounter between Confederates and George Custer near Charlottesville:

> The Yanks were now getting ready to dash upon us, and in another moment they commenced a charge and our little squad, having made the best stand they could, wheeled and ran. There was but one opening in the rail fence which surrounded the field, by which we could escape, and I shall never forget the uncomfortable sound of those Yankee carbine balls as they whistled over our backs when we crowded through the gap. To my amazement they failed to hit a man or a horse, and I turned around after getting through the fence to observe a dozen Yankees within 20 paces, yelling 'Surrender' at the top of their voices. This same party galloped their horses along the fence until they came within easy pistol shot of General Stuart and Captain Grattan, to whom they gave chase. The general seeing that they could not get at him over the fence, cantered along down the lane rather too leisurely, turning every now and then to his ordnance officer and saying, 'Shoot that fellow, Grattan! Shoot him!' pointing to a Yankee who was plugging away at them both. But instead of Grattan shooting him, the Yankee shot Grattan's horse, inflicting a severe wound in his hindquarters and laming him.[7]

In early May, the aim of Federal troops proved to be much better. Charles Grattan was nearby when Stuart was mortally wounded on the 11th. The general died in Richmond the next day. While this led to fresh grief, the Grattans would also mourn one of their own. Peter Minor Grattan had been killed in action at Spotsylvania just five days earlier. Charles lost both a brother and his beloved commander within a week. Poor Patsy lost half of her adult sons—without even having Peter's body. Of the four Grattan men of combat age in 1861, two were dead by the end of spring 1864. The same pattern had occurred with Peachy's two sons, with the youngest killed at Seven Pines in 1862.[8] Similar events occurred in other families; at the beginning of 1864 the Confederacy was running out of human resources. To sustain its hopes, the southern government turned to conscripting seventeen-year-olds and men over the age of forty-five.

At the beginning of May, Patsy Grattan and Lucy saw teenagers called up for duty in the Shenandoah Valley. One Rockingham County man, Major George D. Chrisman, organized part of them into a cavalry unit known as the "boy company." Since more than a few of these seventeen-year-olds ended up with white horses, they attracted public attention as the "White Horse Cavalry." According to the historian John L. Heatwole, the vast majority of the teenagers were farmers. The exceptions were "two blacksmiths, a tanner, a miller and two students."[9] Eleven days later these kids were fighting in a cavalry engagement near New Market.

In May, the Valley was being invaded by some 5,000-6,000 Federal troops led by Franz Sigel. To stop this army, John C. Breckenridge brought two brigades from southwest Virginia, reserves from Staunton, and cadets from Virginia Military Institute. The oldest of the VMI students was not yet 18, and one of Peter S. Roller's sons from Mt. Crawford was just 15.[10] General Imboden harassed Sigel's cavalry and slowed his advance. Breckenridge took the infantry "down" the Valley Pike. Over the next few days, the southern force marched north and attacked Sigel's infantry west of New Market early on the morning of May 15, 1864. After several determined attacks, the Confederate troops captured Yankee artillery and drove Sigel's army from the field. The Yankees fled, leaving their "wounded and dead behind." Among the southern casualties were those from VMI, ten dead and scores of wounded cadets.[11]

The victory at New Market cheered Lucy Grattan and even lifted Patsy's spirits, but drew the ire, of course, of General Ulysses Grant. Grant, who was pushing Lee southward, reassigned the inept general Sigel and ordered his replacement, David Hunter, to begin a new offense in the Valley. For the coming months, Patsy Grattan and her daughters watched the North and South engaged in one-upsmanship along the branches of the Shenandoah. A successful action by one side invariably required avenging by the other.

To the amazement of Southerners, Federal general David Hunter combined reinforcements with Sigel's old units and quickly took the field. The unexpected rapidity of his actions caught the Confederacy off-guard, since it had sent much of Breckenridge's force elsewhere. The task of dealing with Hunter fell to Imboden, as one would expect, and to William E. Jones—an old friend and classmate of Stonewall Jackson. Imboden again fought minor engagements to delay Hunter, and Jones scraped together whatever spare troops he could find. An army would soon be formed in the fields in front of Patsy Grattan's home. On June 2,

1864, John Imboden arrived at Contentment's front door. The general's own account exists,

> I was pressed so hard that I had to ...[retreat] to the south bank of the North River, at Mount Crawford, seventeen miles from Staunton, losing a few men killed and wounded during the afternoon. Hunter [U.S. general David] camped at Harrisonburg.
>
> During the night about two thousand men, sent forward by General Jones, joined me [at Contentment]. To my dismay I found they were not generally organized in bodies larger than battalions, and in companies and fragments of companies hastily collected from Southwestern Virginia, between Lynchburg and Tennessee, and in large part indifferently armed. Indeed, many of the men were convalescents taken from the hospitals, and furloughed dismounted cavalrymen who had gone home for a remount, and were taken possession of by General Jones wherever he could find them, and hurried by rail through Lynchburg and Staunton to the front.[12]

Patsy Grattan and her daughters ordered meals prepared for Imboden and his staff, but he had no time for entertainment. To the dismay of the younger women, the general was struggling to organize the growing army. He recalled, "I spent the entire night of the 3rd in obtaining a list of all these small bodies of men, out of which by daybreak on the 4th I had composed, on paper, two brigades and assigned officers to their command.[13]

While the Confederate army continued to grow around Patsy's home, Imboden wrote:

> General Jones arrived at my headquarters a little after sunrise, and on reviewing my operations on paper, he adopted them, and at an early hour in the morning, the various detachments were aggregated in their respective temporary brigades. During the day, General Vaughan, of Tennessee, with from six hundred to eight hundred of his greatly reduced brigade, also joined us. We now had a force of something over four thousand men, including one regular and excellent six-gun battery, and one...artillery company of reserves, from Staunton, with five guns. Hunter,

with eleven thousand superbly appointed troops of all arms, was only eight miles distant in our front, and [U.S. generals] Crook and Averill, with seven thousand more, only two day's march in our rear; the two bodies rapidly approaching each other, and we between them in the condition I have just described, and with no hope of further assistance. Obviously, our policy was to fight Hunter at the earliest moment and possibly defeat him, and then turn upon Crook and Averill and do the best we could.[14]

It is easy to imagine what General William E. Jones looked like arriving at Contentment. He combined disdain for fancy dress with prickly candor. A writer of the period described Jones as "a small, thin, black-eyed whiskered man; he dressed very plainly, bordering on shabbiness; never shaved, never in uniform, no insignia of office. He had a fine…voice; was misanthropic, despising parade and every man that indulged in it; never courting any man's favor; speaking freely, if not curtly, to and of everybody." The same source goes on to add, "He was cool in a fight, and the bravest of the brave."[15]

While everyone expected to fight a battle at Contentment, it was not to be. To the surprise of Jones and Imboden, Hunter did not attack their small army, but swung around it to the east. Patsy, Lucy and the rest of the family watched the army march away. Lines of infantry disappeared in a cloud of dust to the south and then the southeast. The Confederate forces organized at Contentment would engage Federal troops near Piedmont, just north of Waynesboro, on June 5th. The Grattans at Contentment learned that the Southerners beat back two assaults on their left, before Union troops poured through a gap on one side of the Confederate army. Imboden describes what happened next: They "pierced the line at this point, and striking the right flank of our left wing, doubled the line back on itself, resulting in the wildest confusion and great loss to us. The brave and gallant Jones was instantly killed." The defeat cost the Confederacy over "1,500 in killed, wounded, and captured."[16]

For Patsy Grattan these events were crushing, and Lucy too lost her normal optimism. Generals Imboden, Jones, and Vaughan had used Contentment as their headquarters. Their army of more than four thousand men had camped in fields, destroying the crops. Then almost as suddenly as they had come on June 2nd, 3rd, and 4th the troops marched off. A day later, a hundreds of these men were dead or wounded. Chrisman's company, as one would expect, joined the fighting in a cavalry engagement at Bonnie Doon. Historian John Heatwole notes the consequences, "forty-five boys 'made a desperate stand' against the veterans of the 21st New York Cavalry, and sustained thirty casualties in killed and wounded. This left only fifteen of the boys in an unscathed condition."[17] Although Chrisman would claim that over 150 Federal troops were killed or wounded, the U.S. government simply replaced them—a luxury the Confederacy could not afford. The Civil War was no longer just grinding up young men in the Grattan family. It was butchering teenagers from the neighborhood—people who Lucy's sisters had once played with. In desperation, Patsy worried, "How much worse would it get?"

For the Grattan family and for incalculable number of others, the news only got worse. George Gilmer Grattan, Alfred Colquitt's aide, was shot in the knee at Cold Harbor on June 4, 1864. One soldier in his diary noted the event and yet another recalled it decades later:

Dear Cournel [sic] George B [sic] Grattan

I Have thought for a Long time that I would write to you. I thought of you a lot since the war. And Have Been to Lotz [sic] of Reunans [sic] hoping to Meet with you But I have never Been able to find you. I was one of the six Georgia Litter Co that Bore you from the Battle Field whin [sic] you was wounded shot through the knee goint [sic]. I was the first man that got to you whin [sic] you was wounded. You looked at Me and asked Me what Litter Co did I Belong to. And I told you I Belong to the Six Georgia. And you said that you always said if you was Ever wounded that you wanted the Six Georgia Litter Co to carry you off. We cared [sic] you Down to Surgon [sic] Swan quarters. Surgon Swan Examend [sic] you [sic] Leg and said it would half [sic] to Be amatated [sic] and you said if your Leg had to Come off you wanted to go to the General Horse Pittle [sic] the Anamalance [sic] was sent for. Whin [sic] it come We Put you in it. thin you said Co. A. I want you to go with me I went with you to the General Horsepitttle [sic]. After we got there and took you out I thin [sic] told you that I was away from My Comand [sic] and I must get Back And you said that Right Co. A. GoodBy. I Didnot [sic] stay untill [sic] your leg was taken off. I Expect to go to the Reunan [sic] in Augusta G.A. in November. I would like Ever so much to Meet you there it Has Been about 43 years since we saw Each other. I want you to write to Me as I would like Ever so much to Hear from you. Whin [sic] you write Address your Litter [sic] to W H Harris Sparta G.A. C/O R. W. Moore.

I Remain as Ever   Yours Truly W. H. Harris[18]

The standard medical treatment of the period was, of course, amputation. For George, the experience was especially bitter. Colquitt had already recommended his promotion to colonel. Had he not been wounded, the soldier would have held the highest military rank ever conferred on a family member.[19]

Still another shock awaited the Grattans at Contentment as 1864 rolled on—an event that may have occurred as early as June or as late as September. Whichever month it happened, it ended three generations of slavery. The Grattans' slaves walked down the lane to the turnpike and disappeared. African-Americans left slave owners whenever Federal troops were nearby, making their own personal decision to end bondage. As Federal armies moved further south, passing Contentment, the Grattans' slaves liberated themselves. This occurred on countless farms where white owners claimed to have been "loved" by their slaves. The Grattans never made such dubious assertions.

It is possible to reconstruct from clues some of the character of the relationship between the Grattans and their slaves. The Grattan family at Contentment for half of 1864 was composed of two adults, two teenagers and a child—all but the youngest were women. It seems improbable that they were responsible for most of the dynamics that shaped slavery at Contentment. The credit, or lack of it, most likely belonged to Robert Grattan Jr.

Robert Grattan Jr. changed working conditions at Contentment after he purchased the farm, its new house, and the mill for one dollar in 1827. At that time, the Grattans' holdings were heavily mortgaged and badly neglected. Fields were not in production and the barn "was falling down." His father's mismanagement suggests a place where 17 slaves did little work, at least in farming. The shift in ownership put the slaves in the hands of a driven person bent on saving the family farm. Robert Grattan Jr.'s efforts to restore the soil to production, a primary goal, meant countless hours and endless days of agricultural labor for somebody. The burden for these changes had to have fallen directly upon the Grattan slaves. A grueling work schedule replaced an easy-going one.

Robert Grattan Jr. made yet another change with devastating consequences. As a young person he had explored the potential of land in Ohio and had established himself as a young attorney in West Virginia. In doing this, he copied his parent's generation. Aunts lived as far away as Kentucky and cousins lived in Florida. His own younger brother had even established a successful medical practice in Alabama before an early and untimely death. Life for many Grattans meant leaving the Shenandoah Valley for some new and distant frontier. Given this past, Robert Grattan Jr. wrote in his autobiography: "I am not surprised that men.... should feel a horror at the separation of the families of slaves. The truth is, however, that in neither case is the separation brought about by cruelty but necessity. Though my Father was compelled to part with his slaves, they were never so much scattered as his own children, and I have no idea that they suffered a tenth part by the separation that his own children did."[20] This statement obscures several issues: First, while the selling of slaves grew out of his father's debt, the slaves were still owned by the Grattans when Robert Jr. purchased Contentment. Since his father's stroke followed this event, the sale actually occurred under the son's ownership. It would be understandable, then, that African-Americans held him accountable rather than his father. Secondly, the decision to move away by Grattan men came from their own free will, while the wishes of slaves were not considered. In 1855, Robert Jr. only had eighteen slaves, while in the 1820s he owned seventeen.[21] Assuming that the eighteen reflects a natural increase in population for the period, then the sale of slaves may have involved at least nine human beings and perhaps more than a dozen. The slaves did not love the Grattans, and to make matters worse, the Grattans kept their uncle's horse, Sorrel, as a pet. Slaves worked hard in the fields while Sorrel only carried the smallest of children and then infrequently.[22] The special treatment of a horse naturally generated resentment. If Robert Grattan Jr. physically whipped his slaves or exploited them sexually, that would have only added to their list of grievances. In 1864, the Grattan slaves were given opportunities to leave, and they terminated slavery. The consequences of their action removed servants from the household and workers from the fields, affecting every aspect of the Grattans' lives.

After the departure of the slaves, General David Hunter's campaign in the Shenandoah Valley continued on the heels of the Battle of the Piedmont. Rather than pursuing the fragments of the Southern army, Hunter sent most of his force into Staunton to destroy what they could. Although Yankees made an effort to protect private property, their commander ordered the destruction of military facilities, including "the depot, railroad installations, a woolen factory, government stables, a steam mill, wagon shops, and storehouses."[23] The quartermaster's and commissary were looted by, as Hunter's biographer put it, a "mixed mob of Federal soldiers, Negroes, Secessionists, mulatto women, children, Jews and camp followers."[24]

A few days later, Hunter was in Lexington drawing up a list of buildings to be burned. These included the barracks at VMI, several houses belonging to faculty members, and the home of Virginia governor Letcher. The destruction of the school and the library that had been moved to Washington College [now Washington and Lee University] did not sit well even with a number of Hunter's own officers and men. The Grattans, themselves, despised Hunter's actions. In fairness to him, VMI cadets were active combatants and their school could easily have been regarded as a military installation. Part of the blame belongs to more than just him, for his biographer notes that Hunter acted after consulting his staff. "In later years, through efforts of Senator Du Pont, VMI was compensated by the Federal government for 'the damage and destruction of its library, scientific apparatus, and the quarters of its professors'—but not for the barracks."[25]

Hunter, the Grattans would learn, crossed the Blue Ridge only to find Jubal Early and a small army protecting Lynchburg. Apparently fearful of Early, Hunter ordered his troops to withdraw. By dawn on June 20th, Federal troops pulled back to the Valley. Now short on supplies as well as apprehensive about Early, Hunter ordered his army into West Virginia. A few days later he passed through Greenbrier, and by the end of the month his army was in Charleston, West Virginia. By withdrawing west rather than retracing his route through the Shenandoah Valley, Hunter had unknowingly committed an immense blunder. He had removed all Federal troops from the area and in doing so had given Jubal Early such a wide berth that he could no longer monitor his movements. At the time, the Confederate general's orders were quite explicit. If he could defeat Hunter, he was to cross the Potomac River, enter Maryland, and threaten Washington, D.C."[26]

With Hunter hiding in West Virginia, Jubal Early was able to implement the rest of Lee's plan. The Southern army rested for several days near Roanoke and marched "down" the Shenandoah Valley. This, of course, took them over the path of destruction left by Federal troops. Seeing the burnt shells of VMI and the governor's house, Early labeled these acts as "the deeds of a malignant and cowardly fanatic."[27]

On the 27th of June, Early's army entered Staunton. A day or so later the Confederate force marched down the Valley Pike, camping at Contentment and at Mt. Crawford.[28] It was an amazing sight to the Grattan women—to have been hosts three weeks earlier to Imboden and Jones, only to see them vanquished. Now Lucy's hopes soared as Early traversed an empty Shenandoah Valley. At the time, Southerners hoped to prevent Northerners from winning major victories. If this had continued into the fall elections of 1864, a frustrated electorate might have abandoned Lincoln and chosen someone willing to end the war. Early's campaign also had the potential of pulling Union troops away from Grant and the brutal war of attrition he was waging with Lee.

By June 30th the Grattans would learn, General Early was in New Market and on July 2, 1864, his army marched into Winchester. Just over a week later: "Early's exhausted soldiers appeared before Fort Stevens in the District of Columbia, but the defenders were able to prevent an assault. The Confederate commander decided that he was facing impossible odds....Late on 12 July, Early withdrew from before the capital city, leaving behind looted houses and the burned ruins of 'Falkland,' the home of Postmaster General Montgomery Blair near Silver Spring."[29]

Jubal Early's raid, while it excited the Grattans, raised pointed questions about the quality of Federal commanders. David Hunter had destroyed his reputation, as well, by straying deep into West Virginia and then by not closing in on Early from the west. Quick action by Hunter could have trapped the Confederate army on the north side of the Potomac. General Grant was not about to tolerate timid leadership; Sigel and Hunter were promptly replaced. The new commanders, including Philip Henry Sheridan and George Armstrong Custer, had very different combat records. Sheridan, according to historian John L. Heatwole, possessed a "natural talent for leading fighting men" and a "first instinct...to strike."[30] His aggressive nature was, of course, matched by Custer's.

Grant's instructions to Sheridan were graphic and when they were implemented, they radically changed the Grattans' world. Sheridan was to destroy Early's army and then eliminate the Shenandoah Valley as a primary source of supplies for Lee's army. The local newspaper in Harrisonburg printed his orders after the Civil War. "Do all the damage to railroads and crops that you can, carry off stock of all descriptions and Negroes, so as to prevent further planting. If the war is to last another year we want the Shenandoah Valley to remain a barren waste."[31] Defeating Early, of course, was no easy assignment, but after tenacious fighting at Winchester on Sept. 19th and at Fisher's Hill several days later, Sheridan drove Confederate forces into the southern half of the Valley.

Word of these events reached Contentment as the battered remnants of Early's army fled toward Staunton. For the family, then composed of Patsy Minor Grattan, 54, and daughters, Lucy, 29, Mary, 17, Louisa, 14, and son John, 9, it meant that they had been abandoned to Federal troops. If there was any comfort for the family, it came from the presence of George Gilmer Grattan. The son with the amputated leg had returned to the ancestral residence in late July. Neighbor Peter S. Roller noted the event in a letter, "George Grattan arrived at home several days ago. I have not had time to call on him. I feel very sorry for him."[32]

The events in late September at Contentment were almost as dire as those at Grassy Dale, the elaborate farm less than a mile to the south. When Federal troops reached the Roller place on Sept. 29, 1864, they set out to end its ability to supply agricultural commodities. A few days later its owner described the devastation: "I am sorry to say that the Yankees have burned up all my barns and stables and with them my crop of wheat, oats, hay. I suppose that my loss is about 2000 bushels [of] wheat, 500 bushels [of] oats, and 50 tons of hay." The losses continued because personal possessions were looted. Roller lamented, "...they have stolen nearly all my clothing and stole your mother's linens that she had made for herself and Sally. They have stolen almost everything that they could lay their hands upon." Such treatment had come to many pacifists—hundreds of Mennonites and Quakers losing barns, crops, and livestock—but Peter S. Roller was among the Valley's better-known secessionists. Federal troops searched the house "from seller to garret and made diligent inquires for me."[33] To avoid capture, the Confederate sympathizer fled to Early's camp, some eight or nine miles to the south.

A newspaper article from the 1930s indicates that Contentment received similar treatment. Federal troops arrived at the home, looking for Charles Grattan. Rather than finding him, they found Patsy and her younger children and the disabled George. Recognizing that Mrs. Grattan was a widow, the soldiers obeyed orders and spared the barn. Its contents, however, were probably heaped in front and burned. And then they began looting, stealing even the books in the parlor. In the twentieth century, R. Q. Tenney, a veteran of 15th Vermont Volunteers, wrote in the front of a large Webster dictionary: "This book was taken from the house of one of the F.F.V.'s [First Families of Virginia] about eight miles from Harrisonburg...by the chaplain of the 151st New York Volunteers in the fall of the 1864 while with Sheridan on his raid in the Shenandoah Valley. It was abandoned by the said chaplain for want of transportation, picked up by one James Jackson and from him I procured it. Was taken along on the campaign after General R. E. Lee in the spring of 1865, and sent home from City Point, Virginia, about the first of June, 1865."[34]

The Grattans' dictionary went on to remain in the Tenney family for the next seventy-one years. Tenney was himself, newspaper article explained, "a commissary sergeant. In his duties, he traveled with a supply train and so was enabled to carry the book, heavy and leatherbound."[35] Sometime in the twentieth century Tenney learned about the current location of the Grattans and his family subsequently sold the book to one of Patsy's granddaughters. There is no question that the dictionary came from Contentment since the book included both their name and the name of their farm.

Anger and despair overwhelmed the Grattan home; compared to others though, they had been lucky. Local historian John Heatwole notes, "Mrs. Grattan's status as a widow saved the farm structures from being reduced to ashes."[36] In addition, the mill that had been leased to neighbors remained unscathed. There are two stories about how this came about. Heatwole states that Federal troops used it to grind flour and thus spared it out of self-interest. Peter Roller, on the other hand, says that Yankees set fire to the mill but fled because of snipers. In this version, the Grattan family then put out the fire before damage had been done. Given that Federal soldiers came to Contentment on more than one occasion, it seems probable that both events actually happened.

Federal troops divided Rockingham County into districts and systematically used torches to end agricultural production. Thomas C. Devin with one New York unit reported the destruction around Contentment, moving in a circle from "McGaugheystown" east of Harrisonburg, south and then west. On "September 29, the brigade swung around by Port Republic...Piedmont, and the Valley Pike, to Mt. Crawford." In rapid order, they burned "82 barns, containing hay and grain, 72 stacks of hay and grain, 5 flour mills, 2 saw mills, 1 iron furnace, 1 wagon loaded with grain and 1 wagon of flour, and drove... [off] 321 head of cattle and 20 sheep."[37] The same units continued their mayhem and Thomas Devin described their efforts on Oct. 8, 1864: "Two regiments burnt 115 barns filled with hay and grain, 206 stacks of hay and grain, 18 flour and grist mills, 18,000 bushels of wheat, 1 woolen mill, 2 saw mills, and 60 acres of stacked corn. The brigade also drove ... [off] 290 head of cattle, 319 sheep, and 75 hogs. The railroad depot at Woodstock, containing a locomotive engine and three cars, was also burned."[38] The Grattans watched the smoke rising in the distance, leaving a horrifying trail visible for miles. It is not surprising that the aggregate damage in the Shenandoah Valley claimed in Sheridan's reports exceeded 2,000 barns. One division alone incinerated 630 barns, 47 flourmills, 4 sawmills, and 1 woolen mill between Port Republic and Front Royal. The livestock taken included 1,347 cattle, 1,231 sheep, and 725 swine. Perhaps to Lee's army the worst news was the loss of 410,742 bushels of wheat with a cash value of over a million dollars.[39]

Various southern cavalry units harassed Yankees as this agricultural holocaust unfolded, and Confederate forces returned to Contentment. In early October, Union general Wesley Merritt reported the action near Mt. Crawford: "On the 2nd the enemy advanced and skirmishing took place along my entire line, lasting all day."[40] Maps from the period place Confederate regiments on the banks of the North River, running from the hill west of Contentment, along the fields for almost half a mile, ending at the Grattan house. Southern troops moved from these positions on high ground down the Valley Pike while other units forded the stream at the old stage crossing by the home. For the Grattans, especially for Lucy, these activities must have seemed too little, too late. At Cedar Creek north of Strasburg, Early's starving troops launched a surprise attack on October 19th. When his men stopped to eat Federal rations, the assault faltered. The shattered fragments of his once proud army were driven off by dusk, ending serious military action in the Shenandoah Valley.

The first snowfall of the winter produced a barren, surreal world—white contrasting with the ashes of barns and outbuildings. The slaughter of livestock left an unnatural silence compounded by human sorrow. John Imboden reported on casualties among his three regiments in January 1865. Between May 1st and November 1st, 1864, his Valley cavalry unit lost 643 men, killed or wounded, with 244 men captured out of a force of less than 1, 300.[41] The scale of the suffering was staggering. In her grief Patsy concluded that the war was an immense waste, while Lucy only regretted that the South had not won.

Notes:

1. Charles T. O'Ferrall, *Forty Years of Active Service*.
2. C. E. May, *Life Under Four Flags*, 428.
3. Coles, 91.
4. Ibid., 93. A history of the artillery unit includes George Grattan's own published account of the battle. It is unusual for the seniority of its author and the close proximity between the battle and the publication. Charles C. Jones, Jr.'s *Historical Sketch of the Chatham Artillery* first appeared in 1867.
5. Coles, 160. See page 31 in Mark Boyd's article.
6. W. H. Harris to George G. Grattan, Sept. 15, 1907.
7. Garnett, *Riding with Stuart*, 42.
8. Peachy R. Grattan to John Grattan, Dec. 15, 1879.
9. John Heatwole, *Chrisman's Boy Company*, 15.
10. C. E. May, *Life Under Four Flags*, 430.
11. Ibid., 431.
12. Imboden, "Fire, Sword, and the Halter," 172.
13. Ibid..
14. Ibid.
15. Edward E. Pollard, *Southern History of the War*, 329.
16. Ibid. Also see Edward A. Miller Jr.'s *Lincoln's Abolitionist General: The Biography of David Hunter*, 186-7.
17. Heatwole, *Chrisman's Boy Company*, Addendum, 48.
18. To G.G. Grattan from W. H. Harris, Sept. 15, 1907. Original in the collection of Martha Townes Grattan and George Gilmer Grattan, IV. Grattan's wound was also recorded by Washington L. Dunn in *Confederate Reminiscences and Letters, 1861-1865*. Atlanta: Georgia Division of the United Daughters of the Confederacy, 2001, 82.
19. This explains why Harris addressed his letter "Cournel" [sic] not "Captain."
20. Grattan, "Manuscript of Robert Grattan, Jr," 17-18.
21. Compare the information from 1855 in C. E. May to the Rockingham County Deed Book. (Replacement of the burnt copy.)
22. See Gilmer, *Sketches of Some Early Settlers*, 18.
23. Edward Miller, *Lincoln's Abolitionist General*, 189.
24. Ibid., 195.
25. Ibid.
26. Ibid., 208.
27. Ibid., 216.
28. Cooling, *Jubal Earlys Raid on Washington*, 23.
29. Ibid., 220.
30. Heatwole, *The Burning*, 11.
31. *Rockingham Register*, May 19, 1887.
32. Peter S. Roller to Edwin Roller, Oct. 3, 1864.

33. Ibid.

34. *Fort Collins Express-Courier*, Nov. 14, 1935.

35. Ibid.

36. Heatwole, *The Burning*, 51.

37. *War of the Rebellion*, Series I, Vol. 43, 477.

38. Ibid.

39. Ibid., 442.

40. Ibid., 443.

41. *Rockingham Register*, Jan. 20, 1865.

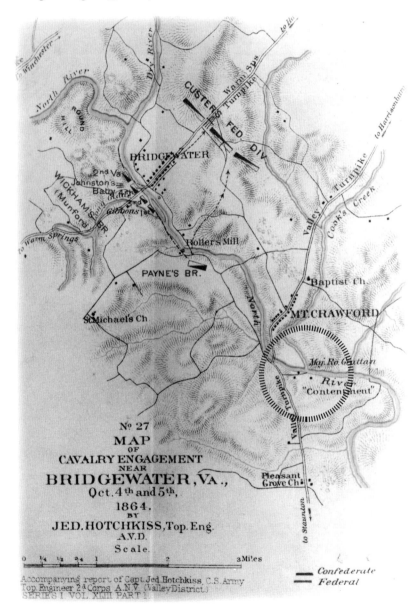

9. Court Square, 1865–1915

At the beginning of 1865, the Grattans graphically knew the impact of Sheridan's army. The destruction of farms in the Shenandoah Valley did more than undermine Southern efforts to send supplies to Lee's army at Petersburg. It also challenged the resolve of many local men still in uniform. Part of the motivation to fight came from the desire of men to protect their families by keeping Federal troops away from the Valley. Now that their barns, outbuildings, and livestock had been destroyed, many soldiers found that they were desperately needed at home. Worries mounted; hungry wives and children fueled desertion rates. The situation was clearly noted in one of the first histories ever written about Sheridan's campaign in the Valley. It quoted an appeal sent from Rockingham County to Richmond. While George Grattan did not write it, he could have expressed the same sentiments:

> Many are without a pound of meat, bread, or anything to live on, to say nothing of firewood. It will require the daily and hourly exertions of the poor and those who have been burnt out to procure a scanty subsistence to sustain life during the winter. When the soldier now in the army learns that his family is sure to suffer, he will become uneasy in his place, and will weigh the duty he owes his family... We have no slave labor [left]. What is to become of a corn crop? What is to become of any spring crop?[1]

Such concerns affected the only Grattan still in military service; Charles had both his new bride to worry about and family at Contentment. Yet he resisted the temptation to create his own leave of absence. To his great relief, orders on February 24, 1865, reassigned him to the Shenandoah Valley.[2] He was given the duty of trying to track down abandoned artillery that Early's army had lost in the preceding fall. It was his last military task.

To the horror of Patsy Grattan, fighting had not ended in the Shenandoah Valley. One last skirmish occurred at the bridge over the North River at Contentment. Philip Sheridan returned to the Valley and offered his own account to the War Department:

> Small bands of guerrillas hovered on our flanks during the day, but no effort was made to drive them off, and no damage was done by them; distance marched, twenty-nine miles.
>
> The march was resumed at 6 o'clock on the morning... [March 1], through Harrisonburg and Mount Crawford... Guerrillas hovered around us during the march, and at Mount Crawford, General Rosser with 200 or 300 cavalry attempted to burn the bridge. Two of Capehart's regiments swam the river above the bridge, charged Rosser and routed him, driving him to Cline's Mill, the advance pushing almost to Staunton; but few of the enemy were killed, 30 taken prisoners, and 20 ambulances and wagons, with their contents, were captured and destroyed; our loss was 5 men wounded."[3]

Federal cavalry chased the last of Rosser's band across the fields of Contentment and "up" the Valley pike. Being the nearest residence to the fighting, the wounded from this tragic farce came to the house for care. The Confederacy was nearing its end.

The surrender of Lee at Appomattox generated a lengthy article in the local newspaper, the *Rockingham Register*. The editor endorsed the general's actions: "Who finds fault with Gen. Lee's surrender of us all? Who? Let him speak out. We do not, because it was unavoidable. Those who had sons, brothers, husbands and other kinsmen and friends in that great and noble Army will say he did what was right and what was just. Suppose he had fought his way out, as he might have done, and had had hundreds and thousands of our friends slaughtered again. Would that have been best? Haven't we suffered enough? Has not blood enough been shed? Who cries for more?"[4] Then the *Register* recommended that Virginians follow the lead of soldiers: "bow to surrender...and observe scrupulously and faithfully the terms of an honorable capitulation."[5] The Grattans, like countless others, were exhausted by war.

Peace gave rise to changes in the Grattan family—a portion of which was foreshadowed by a letter written by George Grattan in October 1863 to his sister Mary, "Dear Mary, Aunt Betty [Eliza Grattan Gilmer] has given me such a startling account of her nieces that I am forced to inquire into the matter. She says they are all so intent upon getting married as soon as the war is over, that she can persuade none of them to go to Georgia with her this winter. Now I want to know in what direction you are all looking. Sister Lucy, I suppose, is making a dead set at Bill Allen, but who are you after?"[6] While we don't know the contents of Mary's response, some Grattan marriages did follow the Civil War. Lucy, courted by a former Confederate officer, George D. Chrisman, married him rather than Allen on 13 November 1867. Mary wed James F. Robertson, and George Grattan married a local beauty, Mary Ella Heneberger, on October 18, 1870.

Well in advance of these weddings, Charles Grattan moved to his wife's home in Augusta County. The Finleys needed him, and at the same time this removed him from his mother and her many regrets about the cost of the war. With the family cemetery in front of the house at Contentment, Charles could not enter or leave it without passing his brother Robert's grave. Besides, he had confidence in his brother George's skills to manage Contentment in spite of his injuries. In the early years after the Civil War, the Grattans possessed assets that far exceeded those of their neighbors—considerable acreage, a barn, and a functioning flour mill.

Life in Augusta County offered Charles a world with fewer Mennonites and German Baptists and less political opposition. In 1870, he opened a law office in Staunton and eventually held several public positions, starting with the school superintendency in January 1879.[7] Eight years later he was appointed to complete the remainder of a term of a local judge who had resigned. Charles Grattan was subsequently reelected to this position for an additional two terms. With declining health, he left the bench on January 1, 1901. It was reported in a Staunton newspaper that he "discharged the duties of this position [county judge] with the utmost integrity and fidelity."[8] Suffering from both heart disease and kidney failure," he died "at 11:30 A.M. on June 20, 1902."[9] At his death at the age of 68, he left five adult daughters, three of who would see more than half of the twentieth century.

Perhaps to the surprise of some Valley residents, the most successful politician in the family after the Civil War was Charles's brother George. Before turning to the career of George Gilmer Grattan, it is important to trace his recovery from the amputation of half of a leg.

Many of George's inner circle who survived the war were non-combatants, women and several children—rallied around George in person and in writing. The correspondents included a sister, a cousin,

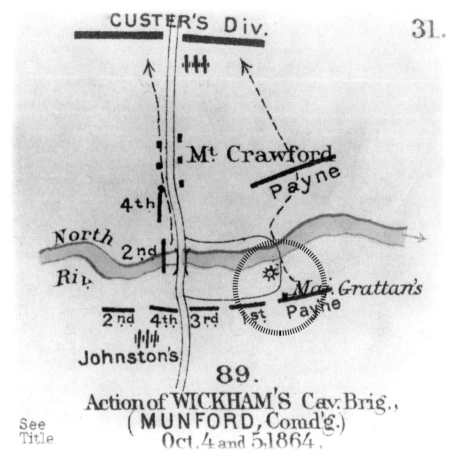

and an aunt. Eliza Grattan Gilmer, the former First Lady of Georgia, sent him four letters that still exist. She began one with the following sentence: "I have been waiting for the last days to see the girls, to write something that might amuse you."[10] Then she proceeded to share news of the social world, who came to dinner, who is engaged to whom, and what is happening in Lexington, Georgia. In subsequent notes Mrs. Gilmer returned to similar themes. Cousin Eliza Gilmer is getting married; Mrs. Shaw played her piano while someone accompanied her on the viola. Reels and jigs followed each other for hours. The tenor of the letters occasionally breaks. On January 4, 1866, for instance, she states that, "Poor Peachy you know lost everything but his land. He is hard at work."[11] A fire had destroyed the business district and countless homes in Richmond. In the third letter, Eliza Gilmer states that she has sold her house and land in Lexington. The funds from the sale are rapidly being used up. The last letter begins,

My darling Child, I am pleased to hear you got safely home. I hope you left special direction about the making up of a leg for your use in Richmond. I now think I shall in a few days have the money to pay for it. I think I will go to Richmond early in April. I hope whilst I am there you will be able to come and get your leg so that I may have the pleasure of seeing you with it on." [After conversing about a number of topics, she concludes] "God bless you. My constant prayer is you may have that faith that will unite you to God and enable you to see clearly your duty and have the strength to perform it….Your affectionate aunt, E.F. Gilmer.[12]

Eliza Gilmer realized that she had lived into a different age. Her correspondence from Virginia indicates an understanding of a world changed. Blacks, as freedmen and women, were no longer forced labor. She commented on April 21st, "The Negroes will not work" and then added, "the white Swists [Swiss], Germans, and etc. will not stay." The latter moved west from Goochland County because "labor is better paid and land [is] cheaper."[13] Three generations of change had not dimmed the family's identity. In noting some of President Andrew Johnson's feisty behavior, Mrs. Gilmer commented: "He must have some Scotch-Irish Presbyterian blood in him."[14]

Although the politics of the period interested the former First Lady of Georgia, time did not permit her to see much of a new era. She died in the summer of 1866, and, contrary to her wishes, was buried in Virginia almost six hundred miles from the grave of the husband who had adored her, George Rockingham Gilmer. Soon after her death, several others of her generation died—notably Martha "Patsy" Grattan in 1869 and the one remaining offspring of Catherine Grattan Gamble, Robert Gamble Jr. Of the many grandchildren of John Grattan, only Peachy would live into the early 1880s. Those people who had firsthand knowledge of the early generations living on the North River were almost gone. Aaron Burr, William Wirt, and the Pen Park Gilmers, including Francis Walker Gilmer, were only names to the younger generation.

The losses to the Gilmer estate from the war explain the delays in funding the most unusual provision in Eliza's husband's will. The former governor stated: "I give and bequeath all property not disposed of by other clauses in this will, namely my land, houses, and lots in Lexington and all notes and bonds which belong to me to form a perpetual fund for educating teachers to teach reading, writing, and arithmetic or other wise form the qualifications of the school master in Georgia."[15] Some $15,000 in pre-war resources would eventually yield interest in the 1880s—funds that the University of Georgia used to support its normal school.

A different cost of the Civil War was the toll it took upon the health of children and the elderly. Many who had been weakened during the conflict died and these deaths were intermixed with economic troubles. Agriculture was disrupted: fences were destroyed and neglected, and most local farmers lost their barns as well as their livestock. Yet even in a cash-starved economy, George Grattan had assets to barter. It would have been easy to trade space in the barn for grain or for labor. Likewise, milling was traded for commodities and livestock. Once things were in order at Contentment, George established a law practice in Harrisonburg.

George Grattan further enmeshed himself in the small town by courting and marrying Mary Ella Heneberger in 1870. The Henebergers were very active in First Presbyterian Church, where Mary's stepmother was the organist. By 1873, the young attorney was an elder in the congregation. Of course this led to a focus on family life away from Contentment, accelerated by the construction of a new home at the south end of Harrisonburg. While the old farm had been left to a number of the siblings, these changes did not keep George Grattan from buying the shares owned by John and Lucy in 1877.[16] With the conclusion of those transactions, the war veteran became the last family member to own the ancestral dwelling. Contentment became increasingly an uncomfortable reminder of the past with the coming of telephones and electricity. Before rural electrification, places like the old Grattan home no longer suited the lives of affluent lawyers. In 1893, without fanfare, George G. Grattan sold the farm, keeping both the family graveyard and the right of access.

The county property records reveal that George Gilmer Grattan bought and sold a large number of pieces of property over many years. As a lawyer he was aware of opportunities for real estate investment, and the attorney made the most of the situation without developing a negative reputation. As the *Rockingham Register* put it in 1879, he was a man with "an untarnished name."[17]

In 1877, George Grattan was appointed to fill the unfinished term of the local Commonwealth's Attorney. In a subsequent bid for office, he handily won the office two years later, defeating four other candidates. Of the 2,431 votes cast, the second closest challenger received only 559, with Grattan garnering 1,056.[18]

It was a turbulent period for George to be launching a political career since Virginia was undergoing dramatic political change. For most of the decade, the nation had been in an economic depression. Booming speculation in railroads in the 1860s gave way to one of the worst economic slowdowns in the nineteenth century. In this environment, the leaders of the state Democratic Party unwisely raised taxes to pay for the Commonwealth's debts and cut funding for public schools. They then added to this mistake by frustrating the political ambitions of William "Billie" Mahone. By rejecting Mahone's bid for the governorship in 1877, the party would unleash a man whose agenda brought change and personal power. It is easy to understand the upper classes' rejection of the former railroad tycoon. The son of a tavern owner he was short, with, as one biographer put it, a "thin and piping" voice.[19] Yet Mahone was adept, with considerable political talent. As a Confederate officer, he had led troops with genuine skill, or as the historian continued, "Mahone was alert, prompt, precise, and contemptuous of indecision."[20] His leadership in 1864 at the Crater at Petersburg helped turn a Federal offensive into a horrific defeat. Consequently, Lee promoted the feisty little man to major general.

Stinging from his rejection by the Democratic Party, Mahone set out to change politics. George Grattan watched him as he adroitly merged several issues—a forty-million-dollar state debt, part of which came from West Virginia from before the war, high taxes, and the cutting of school funding—into the agenda of political action. Raising the banner of "readjustment," Mahone endeavored to reduce or repudiate the debt, cut taxes, and restore funds for education. Such policies were widely popular, especially among small farmers, African Americans, and educators. Mahone's rejection of traditional Tidewater leaders also resonated among residents of the Shenandoah Valley. Political insurrection cut across the sky like a meteor. As one biographer put it, "Under Mahone's leadership, the Readjusters won decisive victories in the 1879 and 1881, elections."[21] The former general then used his power to be elected to the U.S. Senate.

It is easy to understand George G. Grattan's distaste for Mahone. With a flair for wheeling and dealing, the former general began assembling a political machine. As this happened, there was an effort to revitalize the Democratic Party and protect it from Mahone. By searching out new blood and capitulating to many of the demands of Readjusters, traditional leaders endeavored to minimize the senator's power. Real change occurred. The debt was scaled down, with some ten million being assumed by West Virginia and resources were refunneled to schools. As Mahone's frustrations mounted, he tried to form a coalition with Republicans and then switched parties in order to dominate their state machinery. These changes remade politics in the Shenandoah Valley. Some precincts in Rockingham County remained staunchly Democratic while others became the essence of Mahone country. This helps to explain the fractured pattern of the county's voting. Incredibly enough, in the presidential election of 1884, Grover Cleveland carried the county by one vote, 2762 to 2761.[22] Four years later he lost to Benjamin Harrison by only 291.[23]

In August 1883, the *Register* reported that George Grattan was the "unanimous" pick of a Democratic caucus to be the "first man on the ticket for the House of Delegates."[24] The committee easily selected George B. Keezell for the senate, but split over the choice of a candidate for the county's second seat in the general assembly. In a county convention on the 3rd, delegates ratified both Grattan and Keezell and voted on the remaining position. The newspaper went on to champion these candidates: "The ticket elected gives universal satisfaction. Mr. Keezell is young man of character, a prosperous farmer, a fine stumper, and…qualified for the work that is before him. Capt. Grattan is a man of irreproachable character, and for the past four years has been the Commonwealth's Attorney of the county, and would doubtless have been chosen again had he consented to stand for re-election…."[25]

Selection by the Democratic Party did not, however, insure George's victory. While Keezell and Grattan obviously had the support of the *Rockingham Register,* they also drafted a conciliatory platform. It included "no increase of taxation," "no more contests over the state debt," "a tariff that protects, but does not build up monopolies," "continued support for free schools until every child in Virginia of both races has an opportunity to be educated," "no [racially] mixed schools," "economy in all branches of government," "civil service reform," and "opposition to bossism."[26] To counter these goals, the local Readjuster and Republican coalition offered strong rhetoric, playing upon grievances from the past. One inflamed speaker put it this way: "We would no more place the Democratic party back in power than we would turn the criminals out of the penitentiary."[27]

The campaign lasted three months, ending in early November with a result that could rival the 2000 U.S. Presidential election in Florida. Keezell and Grattan lost by the narrowest of margins: 36 votes and 33 votes.[28] Given that some 5,269 ballots had been cast, the differences were minuscule. Although Mahone and his friends prevailed in Rockingham

County, they did not fare as well elsewhere. The Democrats controlled the state senate 19 to 13 and held a larger majority in the house.

Shortly after the election, George Grattan learned about a number of voting irregularities at Conrad's Store—so many that the newspaper stated that an "investigation" was underway.[29] The significance was readily apparent to those who watched politics: The precinct at Conrad's Store, modern Elkton, provided the margin of victory for the Mahone Coalition.

George Grattan used the days following the election to document the irregularities. Witnesses offered testimony that the polls were an hour and a half late in opening, that two of the three election officials left the polling station during the election, and that while these men were gone, ballots were cast by as many as fifty "unregistered" voters.[30] The Coalition candidates, on the other hand, did not attempt, as the *Rockingham Register* put it, to collect depositions. Rather than offering evidence, they "folded their tents and silently stole away."[31]

George Grattan, having led reinforcements into a "fire of canister and shrapnel" at Cold Harbor, was not about to capitulate. With documentation in hand, Grattan turned to the state legislature even though the appropriate committee included part of the Mahone delegation. Perhaps to their surprise, he carried the day. The newspaper reported that the decision of the committee was "unanimous."[32] The house responded by throwing out all the votes from Conrad's Store, rejecting the Mahone Coalition candidates, and seating the Democrat. By any reasonable standard, it was a great victory.

During the legislative session, George Grattan was appointed to a committee on roads and internal navigation as well as to the finance committee. Such responsibilities did not keep him from helping schools. After the senate had passed an act to "authorize district school boards to use district school funds for the pay of teachers," Grattan endeavored to bring it to an early vote. The House Journal noted that George Grattan was successful in moving the topic forward on the calendar, and then added, "On [the] motion of Mr. Grattan, the bill was passed...."[33] The local newspaper observed at the end of the legislative session, "Our representatives...took positions in the General Assembly which reflected great honor upon themselves and credit upon our country. At no period since the war has Rockingham had more earnest, intelligent or honorable men representing her at Richmond, and, we know that all our people, irrespective of party, will concede that they have been honest and capable."[34]

In spite of such glowing comments, local members of the Mahone Coalition were not about to let the matter of the 1883 election drop. Rather than explaining the irregularities at Conrad's Store, they initiated a campaign against George Grattan. According to coalition sympathizers, the man had stolen the election. And once in office, he had voted to let the Medical College of Virginia seize the bodies of the poor and indigent for its research. In fact, the legislation only applied to the remains of convicted felons when they went unclaimed. Rather than consigning them to a potter's field, the bill would have allowed the college to study the bodies for medical purposes. Rather than accepting Grattan's explanations, the opposition simply went on to manufacture new charges.[35]

On November 3, 1885, George Grattan lost his bid for re-election by less than sixty votes. Having endured a campaign of character assassination, the attorney chose to ignore the irregularities in the returns. The nightmare at Conrad's Store was at an end. The observations of the *Register* are worth noting: "George Grattan would today stand as the representative elect in the House of Delegates of Virginia from Rockingham, but for these shameless perversions of plain facts."[36] Perhaps to his surprise, this was not the end of his public service. In 1886, he was appointed county judge—a position he held into the twentieth century.

One of the first murder cases George Grattan presided over reminded him of the medical college legislation, since the corpse of the person executed for the crime went unclaimed. In March of 1886, William Finchum left a house with his brother Preston. Later in the day, William was seen coming out of the woods. Preston's body was later found close to that location with much of the skull blown away. In spite of a number of witnesses, the brother denied ever being near the body. Worse, he attempted to get someone to support a false alibi. Subsequently, the fact emerged that William was having an adulterous affair with Preston's wife. The jury found Finchum guilty of first-degree murder and an appeal to a higher court only reaffirmed the death sentence. At this point, William Finchum confessed. In the confession, the text of which, according to the newspaper, "corroborated...the theory of the prosecution."[37] He was hanged on Dec. 30, 1887. The Finchum family ignored William in jail and his body after the hanging. Not even his mother offered him any consolation, but his brother did claim William's old clothing. The public was excluded from the hanging as well. *The Rockingham Register* explains: "Very few people were in town, knowing perhaps that they could see nothing if they came, as the execution by law is required to be private."[38] In Judge Grattan's day public hangings were outdated.

George Grattan's surviving post-war correspondence includes a letter from Alfred H. Colquitt. The former general and future governor and senator from Georgia wrote him from Charlottesville:

> My dear Capt. I am in Old Virginia again. Precious old commonwealth! She is as dear to me as to many of her native sons. I am on my way to the Rockbridge Alum Springs. Our little boy Alfred has been an invalid for a long time and we have been advised to try the virtue of that water. My family, except for two of the children, is with me or will be with me there, for I sent them from here two days ago while I was further north. I will be there tonight. Now, I wish you would come there and see us without delay. I must not be so near without seeing you. If our little boy improves my family will remain at the Springs all summer, but I shall go back to Georgia in ten days. If you are so circumstanced that you cannot come to the Springs, let me know and I will try to run up to Harrisonburg. I hope however you will find it convenient and pleasant to visit me at the Springs. I have much to talk to you about and a little writing for you to do. Give my kind regards to your mother and the family. Your friend A. H. Colquitt.[39]

Given the years that Colquitt would spend in the U.S. Senate and the close proximity of Washington, D.C., it is safe to assume the former general and his aide-de-camp met a number of times after the war.

At the end of the nineteenth century, George Grattan also read a series of recollections of the Civil War in the local newspaper. The *Rockingham Register* returned to the topic of the war in 1900. The subjects ranged from Hunter's raid in 1864 to Sheridan's destruction of Valley farms later that same year. Of these accounts, that of the burning is the easily the most powerful. A southerner recalled events of his youth, providing evidence of post-traumatic stress:

> We noticed smoke on southward about Harrisonburg. Turning off to the right we rode to the highest point we could find in the crest of the hill. The smoke increased. Tongues of flames some declared they saw. A long, white canvass-covered wagon train was now seen moving along down northward on

Ridge road far across yonder eastward—it passed Linville and was moving towards Broadway.[40]

What could this mean? Too many wagons for a foraging party. What was Sheridan doing? A retreating force never left the Valley pike—the great highway and a magnificent road—so no one thought of retreat. We could not grasp it; it was too bad to think. Falling back along all roads and burning as he comes did not suggest itself to one of our little party; till at last, as we sat on our horses on that lone peak, motionless and horror struck for our country, we saw the awful work come on towards us.[41]

Slowly and relentless it ate its way…Awful tragedy! Barn after barn, at first in the distance as by some invisible hand, takes fire. Then horsemen become visible, threading the fields as the tide rolled nearer, far and wide. On the destroyer comes—spot after spot, belching vast clouds of smoke and flame like Tophet, out there in the Valley beneath us. Some count barns ablaze. I could not count. Some point out the fire fends darting now here, now there; now riding furiously fast cross-fields to a neighboring barn about to escape by neglect. See! he disappears behind it; there, he dashes off again! Oh! we all know what we are expecting next. We are almost breathless. It is but a moment; a little curling smoke, rising upward as if coming from some harmless chimney top when fire is kindled for a meal—a moment more dense clouds, and now all the roof's ablaze.[42]

Our eyes are riveted on the infernal scene! Our hearts, how they pound and hurt us! Oh! Is there no help? Is there no help? **** Time wears on. Now the whole vale is red with fire mile on mile, and enveloped in smoke high overhead, twisting, writhing, dissolving. See! yonder goes right at Broadway Jno. J. Bowman's mill and Sam Cline's great stone barn! A sense of our powerlessness oppresses us. Stupidity lays hold on the mind succeeding consternation![43]

Is the world being set on fire?

Look, men! A barn is being fired near us at our very feet. Furies! 'Quick, let us fall on these burners and throw them in the burning barn,' bursts from several throats at once. March! A start is actually made. Plunging down the hill, we go. But confused cries and sounds reach our ears from another quarter. The tramp of cavalry. 'We are hemmed in, men!' It dawns on us we shall be swept along in front of this awful storm. How shall we slip between the enemy filling every road and visiting every farmstead and seeking stock over all the fields?[44]

In this case, knowing the neighborhood saved them: the Southern soldiers avoided capture by hiding in a small ravine. Obviously more than thirty years had not dimmed the searing memories of the past.

The Civil War left behind a sea of emotions for its aging participants, including George Grattan. Consequently, it may have shocked some Valley residents to find him focusing on the future rather than the past. As county judge, he approved the use of funds to replace the antiquated courthouse in downtown Harrisonburg.[45] When the new building was opened in September 1907, a large crowd assembled along with brass bands from Bridgewater, Mill Creek, and Dayton. As the *Rockingham Register* reported, they were "three of the most creditable musical organizations in the Valley." After stirring music, the article continued, " Judge Grattan opened court in the new courtroom promptly at ten o'clock." Given that he was missing a portion of his leg, "he was supported on the one hand by County Clerk Messerley...and on the other by Sheriff Switzer." Next the sheriff read a formal proclamation to a mixed audience of men and women in holiday attire. Then, after reading and approving the minutes of the last session, Judge Grattan made:

...a brief address to the bar. Without rising from his seat, he said that while no formal opening was intended, he desired to say that nothing contributes so much to good government and the peace of a community as the orderly procedure of its courts. He appreciated as much as anyone the influence of lawyers upon the community in which they lived. To this end, he invoked the cooperation of the bar in the well ordering of all procedures in this court. He pledged himself that in this new room he would do all in his power to effect an orderly administration of justice, and he appealed to members of the bar to aid him in this effort.[46]

Court was then adjourned, and the formal ceremonies continued in the assembly room.

George Grattan also helped create another enduring landmark on Court Square. When First Presbyterian Church outgrew its sanctuary, the old church formed a building committee. George Grattan, as a ruling elder and committee member, oversaw both the purchase of lots on the square and the design and construction of the structure that continues to serve the community to this day. The laying of the cornerstone was described in an August 1907 *Daily News*. Its contents included the following items: "a historical sketch of the church, recently compiled" and "the names of all the officers of the church since its establishment, the names of all its pastors and a roll of the membership brought up to the date of the sealing of the stone.[47]

The newspaper continued, "Other articles deposited were a manual of 'Lexington Presbytery; a history of the Ladies' Church Society, together with a memorandum of the fact that the society had contributed $6,000 toward the erection of the building; a number of coins taken from the corner-stone of the old church; a $500 Confederate note contributed by John Kenney; copies of the newspapers printed at Harrisonburg, and a copy of the *Baltimore Sun*."[48] George Grattan attended the dedication of the sanctuary on December 13, 1908, completing the project. It still helps to give Court Square much of its enduring character.

As the fiftieth anniversary of the beginning of the Civil War approached, George Grattan wrote his own version of the battle of South Mountain, Boonesboro Gap. Since many of the accounts of Antietam ignored or glossed over the nearby engagement, the old soldier felt that this was an injustice to General [D. H.] Hill, to his staff, and to "the brave men who fought with him."[49] On May 20, 1910, he delivered his account as an address to veterans at Robert E. Lee Camp, Number One. The Harrisonburg *Daily News* subsequently published it in 1912.

While this no doubt added to George Grattan's happiness, there were other events that pleased him and his wife. Their three children were married in the early years of the twentieth century. Sons Robert and George Jr. both graduated from the University of Virginia and practiced law. The former did so in New York City, and the latter joined his father's practice in Harrisonburg. Their success was a source of pride.

On the evening of October 30, 1915, the old soldier had a stroke. George Grattan died early the next morning—aged seventy-six, eight months, and eighteen days. It was said in the *Daily News* that "Judge Grattan was surely one of the most distinguished of the soldiers whom our county sent into the service of the Confederate states and his record deserves to be forever perpetuated in bronze or marble in the hearts and memories of our people."[50] George Gilmer Grattan had outlived all of his brothers, his wife, and many of his sisters. Of the great-grandchildren of John Grattan, only sisters Mary, Mrs. James F. Robertson, and Lucy, Mrs. George D. Chrisman, were among the surviving family members. Mary died in 1918 and Lucy followed her in 1923, not many years short of her ninetieth birthday.

Four generations have passed since John Grattan arrived on banks of the North River in 1761. Among the family were a number of distinguished personalities—according to historian C. E. May, at least one in every generation. With their deaths, Contentment entered a long slumber. The subsequent owners of the Grattan estate sold off acreage, let the mill fall into disrepair, and emphasized agriculture at the expense of other activities. The narrowing of economic focus did not guarantee success, and one unfortunate family saw the farm foreclosed. There is also no evidence that the subsequent owners ever used Contentment as a social platform for engaging the wider world. Generals, First Ladies, and members of the state legislature no longer called. The decline was briefly interrupted in the 1930s, when the house was electrified and two rooms were remodeled into a kitchen and another for a bathroom. An extensive front porch and a bay window were also added at the time, and then the condition of the house lapsed again into decline.

The purchase of Contentment in 1968 began a restoration as dramatic as the estate's decline had been. Furniture that had been blocking access to the second floor was removed, and abandoned sections of the home were refurbished. The new owners arrived with a regard for the past and an educational attainment that exceeded that of the Grattans of the past. Contentment was no longer just an oversized, antiquated farmhouse. It became the residence of a distinguished university professor and the home of a woman as vintage Scotch-Irish and as Presbyterian as the Grattans. In much the same spirit, their four daughters were educated to venture forth into the world. The Grattans of old would have heartily approved. It is even possible, if Presbyterian theology is correct, that they rejoiced.

Contentment has been the theater and the stage upon which remarkable families lived—families that treasured their men and their women. It stands on a small knoll near the North River. The Blue Ridge Mountains line the horizon some fifteen miles to the east and the Alleghenies begin ten miles west. Contentment abides in the middle of one of the great valleys of America.

Notes:

1. Pond, *The Shenandoah Valley in 1864*, 200.
2. Trout, *They Followed the Plume*, 157.
3. *War of the Rebellion*, Series I, Vol. 46, 475.
4. *Rockingham Register*, April 21, 1865.
5. Ibid.
6. George G. Grattan to Mary E. Grattan, Oct. 3, 1863. Southern Historical Society.
7. *Hardesty's Historical and Geographical Encyclopedia*, 416.
8. Trout, *They Followed the Plume*, 157.
9. Ibid.
10. Eliza F. Gilmer to George G. Grattan, January 4, 1866. Collection of Martha Townes Grattan and George G. Grattan IV.
11. Ibid.
12. Eliza F. Gilmer to George G. Grattan, April 21, 1866.
13. Ibid.
14. Eliza F. Gilmer to George G. Grattan, Feb. 13, 1866.
15. Florrie C. Smith, *The History of Oglethorpe County*, Georgia, 79.
16. John Grattan to George G. Grattan, Feb. 5, 1877 and Lucy Grattan Chrisman to George G. Grattan, Feb. 5, 1877.
17. *Rockingham Register*, May 29, 1879.
18. Ibid.
19. *Dictionary of American Biography*, Vol. XII, 212.
20. Ibid., 211.
21. *American National Biography*, Vol. 14, 342.
22. *Rockingham Register*, Nov. 3, 1885.
23. Ibid.
24. Ibid., Aug. 30, 1883.
25. Ibid.
26. Ibid., Oct. 25, 1883.
27. Ibid., Aug. 23, 1883.
28. Ibid., Nov. 8, 1883.
29. Ibid., Nov. 15, 1883.
30. Ibid., Jan. 10, 1884. Also see pages 81 and 82 of the *Journal of the House of Delegates of the State of Virginia for the Session of 1883-4*.
31. Ibid., Feb. 14, 1884.
32. Ibid., Jan. 3, 1884.
33. *Journal of the House of Delegates*, 432.
34. *Rockingham Register*, March 27, 1884.
35. Ibid., Oct. 29, 1885.
36. Ibid., Nov. 12, 1885.

37. Ibid., Jan. 5, 1888.

38. Ibid.

39. Alfred H. Colquitt to George Grattan, July 9, 1866.

40. *Rockingham Register,* July 13, 1900. According to John Heatwole, the *Richmond Dispatch* of July 22, 1900, reprinted this article and identified its author as Newton Burkholder.

41. Ibid.

42. Ibid.

43. Ibid.

44. Ibid.

45. "Judge George G. Grattan, of the Rockingham County Court, approved a resolution of the county board of supervisors to contract a loan not to exceed $40,000 for the purpose of erecting a new court house." See John Wayland's *Historic Harrisonburg.*

46. Harrisonburg *Daily News*, Oct. 1, 1907.

47. Ibid., August, 5, 1907.

48. Ibid.

49. George Gilmer Grattan, "Battle of Boonsboro Gap or South Mountain," 3.

50. *Daily News-Record*, November 1, 1915.

Bibliography

Publications:

American National Biography, Vol. 9, 14. New York: Oxford University Press. 1999.

Ayers, Edward L. *In the Presence of Mine Enemies: War in the Heart of America, 1859-1863*. New York: W. W. Norton & Co. 2003.

Baptist, Edward E. *Creating an Old South: Middle Florida's Plantation Frontier before the Civil War*, Chapel Hill: University of North Carolina Press, 2000.

Boyd, Mark F. "The Federal Campaign of 1864 in East Florida," *Florida Historical Quarterly*, Vol. 29, 3-37.

Brown, Alexander. *The Cabells and their Kin: A Memorial Volume of History, Biography, and Genealogy*. Boston: Houghton, Mifflin & Co., 1895.

Bryson, W. Hamilton (ed.) *The Virginia Law Reporters Before 1880*. Charlottesville: University Press of Virginia, 1977.

Bunk, Harry Anthony, *History of Mennonites in Virginia, 1727-1900*, Vol. 1, Staunton (VA): McClure Printing, 1959.

Burton, Lewis W. *Annals of Henrico Parish, Diocese of Virginia, and Especially Of St. John's Church*. Richmond: Williams Printing, 1904.

Chalkely, Lyman *Chronicles of the Scotch-Irish Settlement in Virginia*, Vol. 1. Baltimore, Genealogical Publishing Co., 1980.

Chidsey, David B. *The Great Conspiracy: Aaron Burr and his Strange Doings in the West*. New York: Crown Publishers, 1967 Christian, W. Asbury. *Richmond: Her Past and Present*. Richmond: L. H. Jenkins, 1912.

Coleman, Kenneth. "Restored Colonial Georgia." *Georgia Historical Quarterly*, Vol. 40, 1-20.

Coles, David J. "A Fight, a Licking, and a Footrace: The 1864 Florida Campaign and The Battle of Olustee," Masters Thesis: Florida State University, 1985.

Collins, Linton McGee. "Activities of Missionaries among the Cherokee." *Georgia Historical Quarterly*, Vol. 6., 285-322.

Cook, James F. *The Governors of Georgia, 1754-1995*. Macon (GA): Mercer University Press, 1996.

Cooling, Benjamin T. *Jubal Early's Raid on Washington*. Baltimore: Nautical and Aviation Publishing. 1995.

Coulter, E. Merton. "The Dispute over George R. Gilmer's Elections." *Georgia Historical Quarterly*, Vol. 52, 159-184. Coulter, E. Merton. "Meson Academy, Lexington, Georgia." *Georgia Historical Quarterly*, Vol. 42, 125-62.

Coulter, E. Merton. "David Meriwether of Virginia and Georgia." *Georgia Historical Quarterly*, Vol. 54, 320-338. Davis, Richard Beale. "Forgotten Scientists in Georgia and South Carolina," *Georgia Historical Quarterly*, Vol. 27, 271-284.

Davis, Richard Beale. *Francis Walker Gilmer: Life and Learning in Jefferson's Virginia*, Richmond, 1939.

Dictionary of American Biography, Vols. 3, 7. New York: Charles Scribners, 1931.

Foster, John T and Sarah Whitmer Foster. *Beechers, Stowes, and Yankee Strangers: the Transformation of Florida*. Gainesville (FL): University Press of Florida, 1999.

Furgurson, Ernest B. *Chancellorsville: the Souls of the Brave.* New York: Alfred A. Knopf, 1992.

Gamble, John G. "Reminiscences of Major John Grattan." Archives of the Virginia Historical Society.

Garnet, Theodore S. *Riding with Stuart: Reminiscences of an Aide-de-Camp*. Shippensburg (Pa): White Mane Publishing, 1994.

Gilmer, George G. *Sketches of Some of the First Settlers of Upper Georgia, of the Cherokees, and the Author*. Baltimore: Clearfield Company, 1999.

Grattan, George R. "The Battle of Boonsboro Gap or South Mountain." Archives: James Madison University.

Hardesty's Historical and Geographical Encyclopedia, Special Virginia Edition, Richmond, 1885.

Heatwole, John L. *The Burning: Sheridan in the Shenandoah Valley Charlottesville*: Rockbridge Publishing, 1998.

Heatwole, John L. *Chrisman's Boy Company: A History of the Civil War Service of Company A, 3rd Battalion, Virginia Mounted Reserves*. Bridgewater (VA.): Mountain Valley Publishing, 2000.

Hine, Robert V. and John Mack Faragher, *The American West: a New Interpretive History*. New Haven: Yale University Press, 2000.

Imboden, John "Fire, Sword, and the Halter," in Gary W. Gallager (ed.) *Annals of the Civil War*. New York: De Capo Press, 1994, 169-183.

Jabour, Anya. *Marriage in the Early Republic: Elizabeth and William Wirt and the Companionate Ideal*. Baltimore: Johns Hopkins University Press, 1998.

Jabour, Anya. "Quite a Woman of Business." *Virginia Cavalcade*, Spring 2000, 66-75.

Jones, Charles O. Jr. *Historical Sketch of the Chatham Artillery during the Struggle for Southern Independence*. Albany (NY): Joel Munsell, 1867.

Journal of the House of Delegates of the State of Virginia, 1778-1780. Richmond: Thomas W. White, 1827.

Journal of the House of Delegates of the State of Virginia: for the Extra Session, 1861. Richmond: William F. Ritchie, Printer, 1861.

Journal of the House of Delegates of the State of Virginia for the Session of 1883-4. Richmond: R. F. Walker, 1883.

Kennedy, John P. *Memoirs of the Life of William Wirt*. Vol. 1, Philadelphia: Lea and Blanchard, 1849.

Kennedy, Roger G. *Burr, Hamilton, and Jefferson: A Study in Character*. New York: Oxford University Press. 2000.

Koons, Kenneth E. and Warren R. Hofstra, *After the Backcountry: Rural Life in the Great Valley of Virginia, 1800-1900*. Knoxville: University of Tennessee Press, 2000.

Lewis, S. Joseph Jr. "Letters of William Fisher Plane, C.S.A. to his Wife," *Georgia Historical Quarterly*, Vol. 48, 215-228.

Leyburn, James G. The Scotch-Irish: A Social History. Chapel Hill: University of North Carolina Press, 1962.

Long, Everette B. and Barbara Long, *The Civil War Day by Day: an Almanac*. New York: Da Capo Press, 1971.

MacMaster, Richard K. *Augusta County History:1865-1950*. Staunton (VA): Augusta County Historical Society, 1987.

Manarin, Louis H. *Richmond at War: the Minutes of the City Council, 1861-1865*. Chapel Hill: University of North Carolina Press:1961.

May, C. E. *Life Under Four Flags in the North River Basin*. Verona (VA): McClure Press, 1976.

Miller, Edward A. Jr. *Lincoln's Abolitionist General: The Biography of David Hunter*. Columbia: University of South Carolina Press, 1997.

National Cyclopedia of American Biography. Vols. 1, 11, 21,22. New York: James T. White, 1926.

O'Ferrall, Charles T. *Forty Years of Active Service*. Neale Publishing Company, 1904.

Palmer, Vera. "Gambles Hill: A Rebirth of an Elegant Richmond." Richmond: Ablermarle Paper Company, 1962.

Peyton, J. Lewis. *History of Augusta County, Virginia*. Staunton, Samuel M. Yost and Son, 1882.

Pollard, Edward A. *Southern History of the War*, New York: Richardson and Co., 1866.

Pond, George E. *The Shenandoah Valley in 1864*, New York: Charles Scribner's Sons, 1883.

Priest, John M. *Before Antietam: the Battle for South Mountain*, Shippensburg (Pa): White Mane Publishing, 1992.

"Punishment of a Slave for Murder, Rockingham County, Virginia," *Virginia Magazine of History*, Vol. 7, 303-04.

Reed, V. B. and J. D. Williams (ed.), *The Case of Aaron Burr*. Boston: Houghton Mifflin, 1960.

Robertson, James I. *Stonewall Jackson: the Man, the Soldier, the Legend*. New York: Simon and Schuster, 1997.

Roddy, Ray. *The Georgia Volunteer Infantry: 1861-1865*. Kearney, NE: Morries Publishing, 1998.

Skelton, Lynda Worley. "The States Rights Movement in Georgia." *Georgia Historical Quarterly*, Vol. 50, 391-99.

Smith, Florrie Carter, *The History of Oglethorpe County, Georgia*, Washington (GA): Wilkes Publishing Co., 1972.

Spratt, Thomas M. *Rockingham County Men in Gray. Volume I*. Athens (GA): Iberian Publishing Company, 1995.

Stanard, Mary N. *Richmond: Its People and Its Story*. Philadelphia: J. B. Lippincott, 1923.

"Subscribers in Virginia to Blackstone's Commentaries on the Laws of England, Philadelphia, 1771-1772." *William and Mary Quarterly*, Vol. 1, Series. 2, 183-5.

Trout, Robert J. *They Followed the Plume: Stuart's Staff Officers*. Mechanicsburg (PA): Stackpole Books, 1993.

Turner, Frederick Jackson. *The Frontier in American History*. New York: Holt, Rinehart and Winston, 1962.

U.S. War Dept., comp., *War of the Rebellion: a Compilation of the Official Records of the Union and Confederate Armies.* 128 Vols. Washington, D.C., 1880-1901.

Valentine Museum. *Richmond Portraits: in an Exhibition of Makers of Richmond, 1737–1860.* Richmond: Valentine Museum, 1949.

Van Schreeven, William J., comp., and Robert L. Scribner, ed., *Revolutionary Virginia: the Road to Independence*, Vol. 2, Charlottesville: University Press of Virginia, 1973.

Waddell, Joseph A. *Annals of Augusta County, Virginia.* Richmond: William Ellis Jones, Printer, 1886.

Wayland, John W. *Historic Harrisonburg.* Harrisonburg (VA): Carrier Company, 1973.

Wayland, John W. *Historic Homes of Northern Virginia.* Staunton (VA):McClure Co., 1937.

Wayland, John W. *History of Rockingham County. Harrisonburg.* (VA): C. J. Carrier Co., 1980.

Wayland, John W. *Men of Mark and Representative Citizens of Harrisonburg and Rockingham County.* Staunton (VA): McClure Company, 1943.

Wayland, John W. *Twenty-Five Chapters on the Shenandoah Valley.* Strasburg (VA): The Shenandoah Publishing House, 1957.

Wayland, John W. "The Valley Turnpike Winchester to Staunton and other Roads." *Winchester-Frederick County Historical Society*, Vol. VI, 48-60.

Wooster, Ralph "The Georgia Secession Convention," *Georgia Historical Quarterly*, Vol. 40, 21-43.

Worcester, Samuel A. Plaintiff in Error V. the State of Georgia, Supreme Court of the United States., 31 U.S. 515; B. L. Ed. 483. U.S. LEXIS 489.

Newspapers:

Fort Collins, Colorado. *Fort Collins Express-Courier*

Harrisonburg, Virginia. *Daily News*

Harrisonburg, Virginia. *Daily News-Record*

Harrisonburg, Virginia. *Rockingham Register*

Hartford, Connecticut. *Hartford Courant*

Richmond, Virginia. *Enquirer*

Williamsburg, Virginia. *Virginia Gazette*

Manuscripts:

Colquitt, Alfred H. Grattan Family Papers, Collection of Martha Townes Grattan and George Gilmer Grattan IV.

Dozier, Thomas H. Grattan Family Papers, Collection of Martha Townes Grattan and George Gilmer Grattan IV.

Gamble, Sarah Jane "Reminiscences," Grattan Family Papers, Collection of Martha Townes Grattan and George Gilmer Grattan IV.

Gilmer, George R. "Album," Grattan Family Papers, Collection of Martha Townes Grattan and George Gilmer Grattan IV.

Grattan, Mary Elizabeth, "M.E. Grattan Papers," #2975-Z, Southern Historical Society.

Grattan, Robert, Jr., "Manuscript [Autobiography] of Major Robert Grattan Jr." Grattan Family Papers, Collection of Martha Townes Grattan and George Gilmer Grattan IV.

May, C. E. "The Grattans in Augusta and Rockingham Counties," Grattan Family Papers, Collection of Martha Townes Grattan and George Gilmer Grattan IV.

Roller, Peter S., "Roller Family Papers," Bridgewater College Archives, Bridgewater, Virginia.

Index